PHONICS and WORD STUDY
for Struggling Readers

Correlated to State Standards

Visit *www.teaching-standards.com* to view a correlation of this book's activities to your state's standards. This is a free service.

EMC 3361

Evan-Moor®
EDUCATIONAL PUBLISHERS
Helping Children Learn since 1979

Editorial Development:	Camille Liscinsky
	Mary McClellan
	Ann Rossi
Copy Editing:	Carrie Gwynne
Cover/Illustrations:	Lauren Scheuer
Art Direction:	Cheryl Puckett
Design/Production:	Marcia Smith

Congratulations on your purchase of some of the finest teaching materials in the world.

Photocopying the pages in this book is permitted for single-classroom use only. Making photocopies for additional classes or schools is prohibited.

For information about other Evan-Moor products, call 1-800-777-4362, fax 1-800-777-4332, or visit our Web site, www.evan-moor.com. Entire contents © 2008 EVAN-MOOR CORP. 18 Lower Ragsdale Drive, Monterey, CA 93940-5746. Printed in USA.

Contents

Introduction
What's in This Book? 6
Decoding Strategies student poster 8

Phonics: Recognizing Letters and Their Sounds 9

Consonant Sounds
Overview 10
Pretest: /n/, /r/, /t/, /b/, /l/, /m/ 11
Learn It! /n/, /r/, /t/ 12
Practice It! /n/, /r/, /t/ 13
Learn It! /b/, /l/, /m/ 14
Practice It! /b/, /l/, /m/ 15
Review It! /n/, /r/, /t/, /b/, /l/, /m/ 16
Read It! *Baseball Bash* 17
Apply It! consonant sounds 18

Pretest: /d/, /f/, /p/, /h/, /k/, /v/ 19
Learn It! /d/, /f/, /p/ 20
Practice It! /d/, /f/, /p/ 21
Learn It! /h/, /k/, /v/ 22
Practice It! /h/, /k/, /v/ 23
Review It! /d/, /f/, /p/, /h/, /k/, /v/ 24
Read It! *A King to Depend On* 25
Apply It! consonant sounds 26

Pretest: /j/, /w/, /y/, /kw/, /z/,
   /d/, /f/, /g/, /l/, /s/ 27
Learn It! /j/, /w/, /y/ 28
Practice It! /j/, /w/, /y/ 29
Learn It! /kw/, /ks/, /z/ 30
Practice It! /kw/, /ks/, /z/ 31
Review It! /kw/, /ks/, /z/ 32
Learn It! /d/, /f/, /g/, /l/, /s/, /z/ 33
Practice It! /d/, /f/, /g/, /l/, /s/, /z/ 34
Review It! /d/, /f/, /l/, /s/, /z/ 35
Read It! *And the Answer Is…* 36
Apply It! consonant sounds 37

Long and Short Vowel Sounds and Patterns
Overview 38
Pretest: *a, e, i* 39
Learn It! short and long *a* 40
Practice It! short and long *a* 41
Review It! short and long *a* 42
Learn It! short and long *e* 43
Practice It! short and long *e* 44
Review It! short and long *e* 45
Learn It! short and long *i* 46
Practice It! short and long *i* 47
Review It! short and long *i* 48
Read It! *Amber Gets a Pet* 49
Apply It! vowel sounds 50

Pretest: *o, u, y* 51
Learn It! short and long *o* 52
Practice It! short and long *o* 53
Review It! short and long *o* 54
Learn It! short and long *u* 55
Practice It! short and long *u* 56
Review It! short and long *u* 57
Learn It! sounds of *y* 58
Practice It! sounds of *y* 59
Review It! sounds of *y* 60
Read It! *Bogs Full of Clues* 61
Apply It! vowel sounds 62

Pretest: CVC, CVCC, CVCe patterns 63
Learn It! CVC 64
Practice It! CVC 65
Review It! CVC 66
Learn It! CVCC 67
Practice It! CVCC 68
Review It! CVCC 69
Learn It! CVCe 70
Practice It! CVCe 71

Review It! CVCe 72
Read It! *Luke's Job* 73
Apply It! vowel patterns 74

Consonant Variants and Digraphs

Overview 75
Pretest: sounds of *c, g, s* 76
Learn It! *c* 77
Practice It! *c* 78
Review It! *c* 79
Learn It! *g* 80
Practice It! *g* 81
Review It! *g* 82
Learn It! *s* 83
Practice It! *s* 84
Review It! *s* 85
Read It! *Crazy for Candy Corn* 86
Apply It! consonant variants 87

Pretest: *ch, sh, th, wh, ph, gh* 88
Learn It! *ch, sh, th, wh* 89
Practice It! *ch, sh, th, wh* 90
Review It! *ch, sh, th, wh* 91
Learn It! *ph, gh* 92
Practice It! *ph, gh* 93
Review It! *ph, gh* 94
Read It! *A Whale to Watch* 95
Apply It! consonant digraphs 96

Pretest: sounds of *ch, sh, ci, ti* 97
Learn It! *ch* 98
Practice It! *ch* 99
Review It! *ch* 100
Learn It! /sh/ spelled *sh, ci, ti* 101
Practice It! /sh/ spelled *sh, ci, ti* 102
Review It! /sh/ spelled *sh, ci, ti* 103
Read It! *A Mission to Change* 104
Apply It! consonant digraphs 105

Consonant Blends

Overview 106
Pretest: initial *r-* and *l-*blends 107
Learn It! initial *r-*blends 108
Practice It! initial *r-*blends 109

Review It! initial *r-*blends 110
Learn It! initial *l-*blends 111
Practice It! initial *l-*blends 112
Review It! initial *l-*blends 113
Read It! *Honoring Grandmother* 114
Apply It! consonant blends 115

Pretest: initial *s-*blends; ending blends 116
Learn It! initial *s-*blends 117
Practice It! initial *s-*blends 118
Review It! initial *s-*blends 119
Learn It! ending blends 120
Practice It! ending blends 121
Review It! ending blends 122
Read It! *Stella's Sled Ride* 123
Apply It! consonant blends 124

Vowel Digraphs and Other Letter Combinations

Overview 125
Pretest: *ai, ay, ea, ey; ea, ee, ey, ie* 126
Learn It! *ai, ay, ea, ey* 127
Practice It! *ai, ay, ea, ey* 128
Review It! *ai, ay, ea, ey* 129
Learn It! *ea, ee, ey, ie* 130
Practice It! *ea, ee, ey, ie* 131
Review It! *ea, ee, ey, ie* 132
Read It! *Creatures of the Deep* 133
Apply It! long vowel digraphs 134

Pretest: *ie, igh, uy, ye; oa, oe, ow; ew, ue* 135
Learn It! *ie, igh, uy, ye* 136
Practice It! *ie, igh, uy, ye* 137
Review It! *ie, igh, uy, ye* 138
Learn It! *oa, oe, ow* 139
Practice It! *oa, oe, ow* 140
Review It! *oa, oe, ow* 141
Learn It! *ew, ue* 142
Practice It! *ew, ue* 143
Review It! *ew, ue* 144
Read It! *A Trail of Clues* 145
Apply It! long vowel digraphs;
  letter combinations 146

Pretest: *ea, ui, ou; au, aw* 147	Review It! *b, w* 185
Learn It! *ea, ui, ou* 148	Read It! *Why Did You*
Practice It! *ea, ui, ou* 149	*Sign Me Up for Camp?* 186
Review It! *ea, ui, ou* 150	Apply It! silent consonants 187
Learn It! *au, aw* 151	
Practice It! *au, aw* 152	**Diphthongs**
Review It! *au, aw* 153	Overview 188
Read It! *Caught!* 154	**Pretest:** *oi/oy; ou/ow* 189
Apply It! vowel digraphs 155	Learn It! *oi/oy* 190
	Learn It! *ou/ow* 191
Pretest: *oo; ough* 156	Practice It! *oi/oy; ou/ow* 192
Learn It! *oo* 157	Review It! *oi/oy; ou/ow* 193
Practice It! *oo* 158	Read It! *Scout Gets Out!* 194
Review It! *oo* 159	Apply It! diphthongs 195
Learn It! *ough* 160	
Practice It! *ough* 161	**Syllable Patterns**
Review It! *ough* 162	Overview 196
Read It! *Foolproof Cooking* 163	**Pretest:** syllables; syllable patterns 197
Apply It! variant vowel digraphs;	Learn It! syllables 198
letter combinations 164	Practice It! syllable patterns 199
	Review It! multisyllabic words 200
***R*-Controlled Vowels**	Learn It! double consonants 201
Overview 165	Practice It! double consonants 202
Pretest: *ar, or, er, ir, ur* 166	Review It! double consonants 203
Learn It! *ar, or, er, ir, ur* 167	Read It! *Klue, Secret Agent* 204
Practice It! *ar, or, er, ir, ur* 168	Apply It! syllable patterns 205
Review It! *ar, or, er, ir, ur* 169	
Read It! *A Powerful Punch!* 170	**Pretest:** syllables with schwa 206
Apply It! *r*-controlled vowels 171	Learn It! unstressed syllables 207
	Practice It! initial schwa 208
Silent Consonants	Review It! initial schwa 209
Overview 172	Learn It! final schwa + /n/ or /l/ 210
Pretest: *h, l, t, c, g, k, b, w* 173	Practice It! final schwa + /n/ or /l/ 211
Learn It! *h, l* 174	Review It! final schwa + /n/ or /l/ 212
Practice It! *h, l* 175	Learn It! final schwa + /r/ 213
Review It! *h, l* 176	Practice It! final schwa + /r/ 214
Learn It! *t, c* 177	Review It! final schwa + /r/ 215
Practice It! *t, c* 178	Read It! *Lauren's Horrible Day* 216
Review It! *t, c* 179	Apply It! unstressed syllables 217
Learn It! *g, k* 180	
Practice It! *g, k* 181	
Review It! *g, k* 182	
Learn It! *b, w* 183	
Practice It! *b, w* 184	

Word Study: Recognizing Word Parts and Their Meanings 218

Plurals and Inflectional Endings

Overview 219
Pretest: noun and verb endings 220
Learn It! -s, -es 221
Practice It! -s, -es 222
Review It! -s, -es 223
Learn It! other plural forms 224
Practice It! other plural forms 225
Review It! other plural forms 226
Learn It! -ed, -ing 227
Practice It! -ed, -ing 228
Review It! -ed, -ing 229
Learn It! irregular verbs 230
Practice It! irregular verbs............................. 231
Review It! irregular verbs 232
Read It! *The Shopping Trip* 233
Apply It! noun and verb endings 234

Possessives and Contractions

Overview 235
Pretest: singular and plural possessives; contractions 236
Learn It! possessives 237
Practice It! possessives 238
Review It! possessives 239
Learn It! contractions 240
Practice It! contractions 241
Review It! contractions 242
Read It! *What'll He Do Next?* 243
Apply It! possessives; contractions 244

Affixes and Compound Words

Overview 245
Pretest: pre-, re-, im-, in-, un-, dis-, mis-, non-, over- 246
Learn It! pre–, re–, im–, in–, un– 247
Practice It! pre–, re–, im–, in–, un– 248
Review It! pre–, re–, im–, in–, un– 249
Learn It! dis–, mis–, non–, over– 250
Practice It! dis–, mis–, non–, over– 251
Review It! dis–, mis–, non–, over– 252
Read It! *A Misadventure* 253
Apply It! prefixes 254

Pretest: –ly, –or, –er, –est, –less, –ness, –able ... 255
Learn It! –ly, –or, –er, –est 256
Practice It! –ly, –or, –er, –est 257
Review It! –ly, –or, –er, –est 258
Learn It! –able, –less, –ness 259
Practice It! –able, –less, –ness 260
Review It! –able, –less, –ness 261
Learn It! compound words 262
Practice It! compound words 263
Review It! compound words 264
Read It! *A Desert Birthday* 265
Apply It! affixes and compound words 266

High-Frequency Words

Overview 267
Word lists 268

Answer Key 277

What's in This Book?

Here's what you'll find in *Phonics and Word Study for Struggling Readers*:

Teacher Resources

Section Overviews for the Teacher
For each broad section of skills, an overview page explains the targeted skills and suggests age-appropriate ways to introduce the skills to students.

Pretests
The 24 pretests, presented in standardized-test format, help you assess each student's competency with the targeted skills. You can then differentiate instruction by using only those practice pages appropriate to the needs of each student.

High-Frequency Words
Students' ability to read high-frequency words quickly and accurately is critical to developing fluency and confidence. The 240 high-frequency words at the back of this book, compiled from the well-respected *Dolch Basic Sight Vocabulary* and *Fry's Instant Words*, are provided in lists of 15 for students to practice and master. These words, in addition to phonics instruction, will help students access text and develop their decoding skills.

- Recording spaces to track progress and improve speed
- Cover page to make a booklet for convenient and ongoing review

Student Practice Pages

The practice pages for each targeted skill follow all the steps of a pedagogically-sound phonics lesson.

Learn It!
- Rule box explaining the targeted skills
- Words to decode out loud
- Targeted skills practice

Practice It!
- Words to decode out loud
- Fun word game

Review It!
- Cloze activity that reviews the targeted skills
- Presents words in meaningful context

Read It!
An engaging illustrated story provides a meaningful opportunity to read words with the targeted skills in context.

Apply It!
Following the story, students apply their knowledge of the targeted skills.
- Questions on phonics or word study
- Comprehension and critical thinking
- Oral reading to build fluency

Decoding Strategies Student Poster
Make a copy of the poster on page 8 for each student, or display the poster prominently in the classroom.

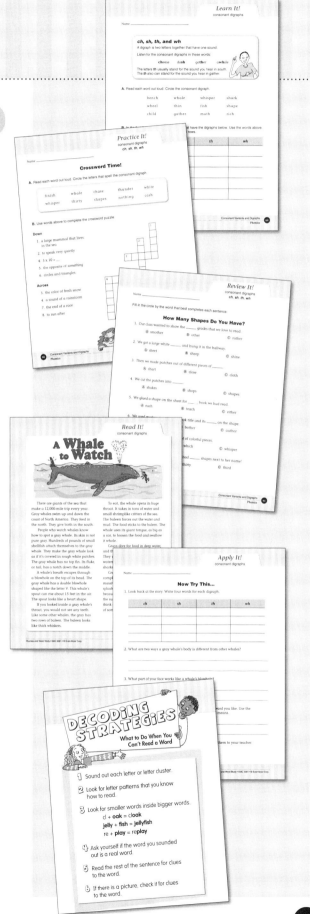

Phonics and Word Study • EMC 3361 • © Evan-Moor Corp.

DECODING STRATEGIES

What to Do When You Can't Read a Word

1. Sound out each letter or letter cluster.

2. Look for letter patterns that you know how to read.

3. Look for smaller words inside bigger words.

    cl + **oak** = cl**oak**

    jelly + **fish** = **jellyfish**

    re + **play** = re**play**

4. Ask yourself if the word you sounded out is a real word.

5. Read the rest of the sentence for clues to the word.

6. If there is a picture, check it for clues to the word.

Recognizing Letters and Their Sounds

Consonant Sounds 10

Long and Short Vowel Sounds and Patterns 38

Consonant Variants and Digraphs 75

Consonant Blends 106

Vowel Digraphs and Other Letter Combinations 125

R-Controlled Vowels 165

Silent Consonants 172

Diphthongs 188

Syllable Patterns 196

Consonant Sounds

b, d, f, h, j, k, l, m, n, p, q, r, t, v, w, x, y, z

Overview
The purpose of the **Consonant Sounds** section is to help students review, a few at a time, 18 consonant sounds and the letters used to represent them. Most students will be familiar with these sounds, but because other phonics skills build on the knowledge of them, students will benefit from a review.

Teaching Tips
You may want to use the following techniques to introduce the concepts in this section:

Letter/Sound Relationships *pages 12–32*
- Encourage students to use the "sounding out" strategy in decoding words. When students see a consonant, they should think about the sound that letter stands for and sound out the word. Model the strategy: Write the letter **b** on the board, and then write /**b**/ next to it. Explain that the **b** has the /**b**/ sound heard at the beginning of *boy*. Call attention to the slashes used to differentiate a sound from a letter.

- Introduce, in alphabetical order, the 18 consonants covered in this section. Write each letter's sound next to it. Have students determine one or two key words for remembering the sound. Encourage students to choose words that are meaningful to them, such as their names and favorite foods. For example, for /**b**/, *Becky* and *bananas*.

- Bring alphabet books to class to reinforce letters and their sounds. There are many sophisticated versions that appeal to older students, such as *The Skull Alphabet Book* and *The Extinct Alphabet Book*, both by Jerry Pallotta.

Double Consonant Sounds *pages 33–37*
Explain to students that once they recognize consonants and their sounds, they can read words that end with double consonants. Point out that in most cases, a double consonant has the same sound as a single consonant. For example, the /**d**/ sound in *ad* is the same as the /**d**/ sound in *add*.

Rule Breakers
While most consonants have the same sound in different words, some consonants' sounds vary. The variant sounds of *c*, *g*, and *s* will be addressed in the **Consonant Variants** section, pages 77–87. Below are points relevant to letters covered in this section:

- The letter **q** almost always represents the /**k**/ sound and is usually followed by the letter **u**. Students will review the spelling/sound pattern of **qu** = /**kw**/, as in *quick*.

- Although the letter **x** has several sounds (such as /**z**/ in *anxiety*, /**k**/ in *excite*, /**gz**/ in *exact*), students will review only the /**ks**/ sound at the end of a word, as in *box*.

Pretest

consonant sounds
/n/, /r/, /t/, /b/, /l/, /m/

Name _____

A. Name the picture. Fill in the circle under the sound you hear at the **beginning**.

1.

/r/ /m/ /t/
Ⓐ   Ⓑ   Ⓒ

2.

/r/ /b/ /l/
Ⓐ   Ⓑ   Ⓒ

3.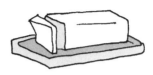

/r/ /b/ /t/
Ⓐ   Ⓑ   Ⓒ

4.

/b/ /r/ /t/
Ⓐ   Ⓑ   Ⓒ

5.

/l/ /r/ /n/
Ⓐ   Ⓑ   Ⓒ

6.

/m/ /r/ /n/
Ⓐ   Ⓑ   Ⓒ

B. Name the picture. Fill in the circle under the sound you hear at the **end**.

1.

/t/ /r/ /l/
Ⓐ   Ⓑ   Ⓒ

2.

/m/ /l/ /n/
Ⓐ   Ⓑ   Ⓒ

3.

/m/ /r/ /n/
Ⓐ   Ⓑ   Ⓒ

4.

/r/ /l/ /p/
Ⓐ   Ⓑ   Ⓒ

5.

/m/ /r/ /b/
Ⓐ   Ⓑ   Ⓒ

6.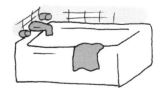

/b/ /t/ /p/
Ⓐ   Ⓑ   Ⓒ

Learn It!
consonant sounds

Name _____

The Sounds of /n/, /r/, and /t/

Of the 26 letters in the alphabet, 21 are called consonants. The letters **n**, **r**, and **t** are consonants. Each stands for a sound.

Listen for the **/n/**, **/r/**, and **/t/** sounds in the words below.

Beginning		End	
name	**n**est	pe**n**	seve**n**
ring	**r**ude	dea**r**	fa**r**
take	**t**oss	ho**t**	lef**t**

A. Write letters to form the words listed above. Then read each word out loud.

n __ __ __   __ __ __ r   t __ __ __   __ __ __ __ n

__ __ n   __ __ t   r __ __ __   __ __ r

t __ __ __   n __ __ __   r __ __ __   __ __ __ t

B. In each box, write a word that begins or ends with the sound.
In the first two rows, choose from the words you formed above.
In the last two rows, add your own words.

	/n/	/r/	/t/
at the beginning			
at the end			
at the beginning			
at the end			

Practice It!
consonant sounds
/n/, /r/, /t/

Name _____

What Am I?

A. Read each word out loud. Listen for the sound of **/n/**, **/r/**, or **/t/** at the beginning and end. Circle the letter that stands for the sound.

name	left	tail	rude
ten	spot	nose	dear

B. Use the words above to answer the riddles.

1. I am next in line after nine.   _____

2. I run without feet.   _____

3. I am never right.   _____

4. I do not look good on a new shirt.   _____

5. I am always first, last, and middle.   _____

6. I am not nice.   _____

7. I wag to say *yes*.   _____

8. I start a letter you write.   _____

C. Write a riddle for the word *tent*.

_____

_____

Learn It!
consonant sounds

Name _____

The Sounds of /b/, /l/, and /m/

The letters **b**, **l**, and **m** are consonants. Each letter stands for a sound.

Listen for the **/b/**, **/l/**, and **/m/** sounds in the words below.

Beginning		End	
band	**b**utter	cu**b**	ri**b**
ladder	**l**ist	nai**l**	rea**l**
meat	**m**ess	tea**m**	hu**m**

A. Write letters to form the words listed above. Then read each word out loud.

l __ __ __ __ __   b __ __ __ __   __ __ __ l   __ __ b

b __ __ __ __ __   __ __ __ m   l __ __ __   __ __ m

m __ __ __   __ __ __ l   m __ __ __   __ __ b

B. In each box, write a word that begins or ends with the sound.
In the first two rows, choose from the words you formed above.
In the last two rows, add your own words.

	/b/	/l/	/m/
at the beginning			
at the end			
at the beginning			
at the end			

Practice It!
consonant sounds
/b/, /l/, /m/

What's Missing?

A. Read each word out loud. Listen for the sound of **/b/**, **/l/**, or **/m/** at the beginning or end. Circle the letter that stands for the sound.

> lift   mind   butter   living   pencil
>
> sum   bike   main   rub   mitt

B. Write *b*, *l*, or *m* to spell the word that goes with the clue. Then read each word out loud.

1. the meat of a pig   ha__
2. not on time   __ate
3. a bone in your chest   ri__
4. a game   __aseball
5. to take a risk   __old
6. letters and cards   mai__
7. another name for *mom*   __other
8. a bed for a baby   cri__
9. at the end   __ast
10. used to buy things   __oney

Review It!

consonant sounds
/n/, /r/, /t/, /b/, /l/, /m/

Name _____

Fill in the circle by the word that best completes each sentence.

Tanika's Dogs

1. Tanika _____ working with dogs.
   - Ⓐ lists
   - Ⓑ lifts
   - Ⓒ likes

2. She likes to toss a ball _____ for the dogs to get.
   - Ⓐ for
   - Ⓑ far
   - Ⓒ lift

3. She also _____ dogs to do what she says.
   - Ⓐ tails
   - Ⓑ trains
   - Ⓒ takes

4. The dogs heel when Tanika says to stay _____.
   - Ⓐ near
   - Ⓑ far
   - Ⓒ dear

5. The dogs sit and _____ for a treat.
   - Ⓐ wait
   - Ⓑ run
   - Ⓒ turn

6. They bark to _____ if danger is near.
   - Ⓐ warm
   - Ⓑ warn
   - Ⓒ nest

7. The dogs do not _____ others.
   - Ⓐ bird
   - Ⓑ back
   - Ⓒ bite

8. Tanika feeds the dogs _____.
   - Ⓐ mess
   - Ⓑ meat
   - Ⓒ most

Read It!
consonant sounds

BASEBALL BASH

Lee and Mike knew they shouldn't. But they did it anyway. The boys played ball in the house. Mike got to try out his new mitt.

The boys tossed the ball back and forth a few times. Then Lee turned and looked left. He sent the ball with a spin to the right. The ball went past Mike and into the living room. He ran and jumped. Too late! The ball hit a plant. It smashed onto the tile floor.

"Now look what you did!" yelled Mike.

Lee rushed to clean up the dirt and the broken pot. Mike picked up the plant. They didn't hear the door open.

"What are you doing with that plant?" Mom asked. She was just getting home.

"It looks too big for its pot," Mike said. "We thought we'd replant it."

"Really?" asked Mom. "When did you boys start liking plants?" Mom's lips showed a bit of a smile. She saw a baseball where the pot once stood.

"When we started tossing a ball in the house," said Mike. "Sorry, Mom. Let's take care of this plant, Lee. It needs a new pot."

Mom handed the baseball to Lee. "And this ball needs a new park," she said.

Apply It!
consonant sounds

Name _____

Now Try This...

1. Look back at the story. Write three words that **begin** with each sound.

/r/			
/l/			
/b/			
/m/			

2. Write three words from the story that **end** with each sound.

/n/			
/t/			

3. How did Mom know that Mike and Lee played ball in the house?
   _____
   _____

4. What could be a reason why the boys played ball in the house?
   _____
   _____

5. What is Mom telling the boys in the last sentence?
   _____
   _____

6. Practice reading the last four paragraphs in the story. Then read them to your teacher.

Pretest
consonant sounds
/d/, /f/, /p/, /h/, /k/, /v/

Name _____

A. Name each picture. Fill in the circle under the sound you hear at the **beginning**.

1.

   /v/   /f/   /h/
   Ⓐ   Ⓑ   Ⓒ

2.

   /v/   /p/   /k/
   Ⓐ   Ⓑ   Ⓒ

3.

   /f/   /p/   /v/
   Ⓐ   Ⓑ   Ⓒ

4.

   /d/   /f/   /h/
   Ⓐ   Ⓑ   Ⓒ

5.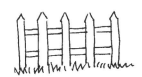

   /k/   /f/   /v/
   Ⓐ   Ⓑ   Ⓒ

6.

   /v/   /h/   /p/
   Ⓐ   Ⓑ   Ⓒ

B. Name each picture. Fill in the circle under the sound you hear at the **end**.

1.

   /k/   /v/   /h/
   Ⓐ   Ⓑ   Ⓒ

2.

   /p/   /v/   /d/
   Ⓐ   Ⓑ   Ⓒ

3.

   /f/   /p/   /k/
   Ⓐ   Ⓑ   Ⓒ

4.

   /p/   /v/   /f/
   Ⓐ   Ⓑ   Ⓒ

5.

   /f/   /v/   /g/
   Ⓐ   Ⓑ   Ⓒ

6.

   /d/   /p   /k/
   Ⓐ   Ⓑ   Ⓒ

Consonant Sounds
Phonics

Learn It!
consonant sounds

Name _____

The Sounds of /d/, /f/, and /p/

Remember, of the 26 letters in the alphabet, 21 are called consonants. The letters **d**, **f**, and **p** are consonants. Each stands for a sound.

Listen for the **/d/**, **/f/**, and **/p/** sounds in the words below.

Beginning		End	
dash	**d**uck	col**d**	her**d**
farm	**f**ence	el**f**	lea**f**
part	**p**ush	hel**p**	shee**p**

A. Write letters to form the words in the list above. Then read each word out loud.

   __ __ f   f __ __ __   d __ __ __   p __ __ __

   __ __ __ p   __ __ __ d   f __ __ __ __   __ __ __ d

   d __ __ __   __ __ __ __ p   p __ __ __   __ __ __ f

B. In each box, write a word that begins or ends with the sound. In the first two rows, choose from the words you formed above. In the last two rows, add your own words.

	/d/	/f/	/p/
at the beginning			
at the end			
at the beginning			
at the end			

Practice It!
consonant sounds
/d/, /f/, /p/

Name _____

Mixed-Up Words

A. Read each word out loud. Listen for the sound of **/d/**, **/f/**, or **/p/** at the beginning or end. Circle the letter that stands for the sound.

> fact   shelf   farm   dash
> part   stamp   bold   sheep

B. Unscramble the letters to form words listed above. Write the words on the lines.

1. mfar   _____ _____ _____ _____
2. phese   _____ _____ _____ _____ _____
3. trap   _____ _____ _____ _____
4. elhfs   _____ _____ _____ _____ _____
5. tcaf   _____ _____ _____ _____

C. Unscramble the circled letters above to answer the clue.

I sit in a corner and go around the world.

I am a _____ _____ _____ _____ _____ .

Name _____

Learn It!
consonant sounds

The Sounds of /h/, /k/, and /v/

The letters **h**, **k**, and **v** are consonants. Each stands for a sound.

Listen for the **/h/** sound at the beginning of these words:
   hang   head   herd   hope

Listen for the **/v/** sound at the beginning or the end of these words:
   vase   visit   five   love

Listen for the **/k/** sound at the beginning of these words:
   keep   king

The **/k/** sound at the end of a word can be spelled with **ck** or **k**.
Listen for the **/k/** sound at the end of these words:
   fork   snack

A. Write letters to form the words above. Then read each word out loud.

k __ __ __   h __ __ __   h __ __ __   __ __ v __

v __ __ __ __   __ __ __ k   k __ __ __   h __ __ __

__ __ v __   v __ __ __   __ __ __ ck   h __ __ __

B. In the first two rows, write words that show where each sound is heard.
Use the words you formed above. In the last two rows, add your own words.

Begins with the /h/ sound	Begins or ends with the /k/ sound	Begins or ends with the /v/ sound

Practice It!
consonant sounds
/h/, /k/, /v/

Name _____

Crossword Time!

A. Read each word out loud. Listen for the sound of **/h/**, **/k/**, or **/v/** at the beginning or end. Circle the letters that have those sounds.

king	glove	snack	visit
hang	kite	herding	vase

B. Use the words above to complete the crossword puzzle.

Across

1. food eaten between meals
5. a thing that holds flowers
7. moving animals from place to place
8. a man who rules a land

Down

2. a toy you can fly
3. a cover for a hand
4. to put up a picture
6. to go see someone

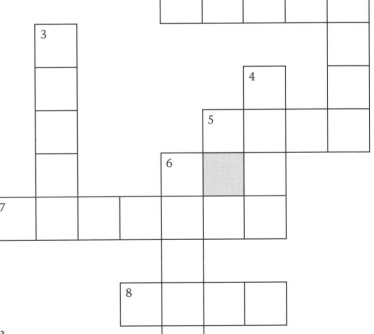

Review It!

consonant sounds
/d/, /f/, /p/, /h/, /k/, /v/

Name _____

Fill in the circle by the word that best completes each sentence.

Family Farm

1. Vic and his family run a small _____.

    Ⓐ farm   Ⓑ fan   Ⓒ family

2. They keep fat hogs inside big _____.

    Ⓐ parks   Ⓑ tents   Ⓒ pens

3. Horses, cows, and _____ are behind a fence.

    Ⓐ herd   Ⓑ sheep   Ⓒ frogs

4. Vic likes the white _____ that swims in the pond.

    Ⓐ truck   Ⓑ herd   Ⓒ duck

5. Vic's job is to _____ the hens.

    Ⓐ push   Ⓑ fence   Ⓒ feed

6. He wears a _____ as he tosses the seeds.

    Ⓐ brave   Ⓑ glove   Ⓒ hand

7. Vic's dogs, Mack and Cheese, _____ the cows in the field.

    Ⓐ pull   Ⓑ herd   Ⓒ fence

8. The dogs _____ all over the farm as they herd the cows.

    Ⓐ dash   Ⓑ drive   Ⓒ leave

Read It!
consonant sounds

A King to Depend On

Val was a city boy. This was his first visit to a farm. Uncle Fred and Pete had lots of animals. Val hoped they had a horse. He always wanted to ride one.

Pete showed Val the farm. King, the family's dog, followed at their heels. After a long walk, Val saw a horse standing behind a fenced area.

"That's Herman," said Pete. "I'll bring him over to you."

Val sat on the fence. He watched Pete slip a rope around the horse's neck. Pete led the horse over.

"Can I ride him?" Val asked.

"Ever ride before?" asked Pete.

"Nope," said Val.

"I'll need to show you what to do. I'll ask Dad if it's okay," said Pete. He went off to find Uncle Fred.

"How hard can it be to ride a horse?" thought Val. He pulled himself from the fence onto the horse's back.

"That was easy," thought Val. He tapped the horse's sides with his heels. Herman began to trot. Val went up and down like a jumping frog. Riding a horse hurt! Then Herman saw that the gate was open. Off they went.

"Help!" Val cried with fright.

"Hang on!" yelled Uncle Fred. "King will get you."

King dashed after the runaway horse. The dog darted back and forth in front of Herman. The horse slowed. Then he turned and headed back.

Pete helped Val down off the horse.

"Good thing King's a herding dog," said Uncle Fred. "If an animal gets too far, King brings it back home. We can always depend on King."

Val hugged the dog. "Horses are okay, but this King rules!" he said.

Apply It!
consonant sounds

Name _____

Now Try This...

1. Look back at the story. Write four words that **begin** with each sound.

/f/				
/h/				

2. Write four words from the story that **end** with each sound.

/p/				
/d/				

3. What could be a reason why Val got on Herman?

   _____

   _____

4. The story says, "Val went up and down like a jumping frog." Complete the sentence in another way:

   Val went up and down like a _____

   _____.

5. Do you think Val will try to ride Herman again? Why or why not?

   _____

   _____

6. Practice reading two paragraphs in the story. Then read them to your teacher.

Pretest

consonant sounds
/j/, /w/, /y/, /kw/, /z/,
/d/, /f/, /g/, /l/, /s/

Name _____

A. Name each picture. Fill in the circle under the sound you hear at the **beginning**.

1.
/z/ /x/ /y/
Ⓐ Ⓑ Ⓒ

2.
/v/ /w/ /r/
Ⓐ Ⓑ Ⓒ

3.
/y/ /j/ /z/
Ⓐ Ⓑ Ⓒ

4.
/kw/ /n/ /z/
Ⓐ Ⓑ Ⓒ

5.
/b/ /z/ /w/
Ⓐ Ⓑ Ⓒ

6.
/r/ /y/ /j/
Ⓐ Ⓑ Ⓒ

B. Name each picture. Fill in the circle under the sound you hear at the **end**.

1.
used for drinking
/g/ /s/ /l/
Ⓐ Ⓑ Ⓒ

2.
it holds water
/l/ /w/ /z/
Ⓐ Ⓑ Ⓒ

3.
the sound of a bee
/z/ /r/ /j/
Ⓐ Ⓑ Ⓒ

4.
to smell
/ks/ /g/ /f/
Ⓐ Ⓑ Ⓒ

5.
laid by a hen
/g/ /x/ /y/
Ⓐ Ⓑ Ⓒ

6.
to get a sum
/s/ /j/ /d/
Ⓐ Ⓑ Ⓒ

Learn It!
consonant sounds

Name _____

The Sounds of /j/, /w/, and /y/

Of the 26 letters in the alphabet, 21 are called consonants. The letters **j** and **w** are consonants. Sometimes the letter **y** stands for a consonant sound.

Listen for the **/j/, /w/,** and **/y/** sounds at the beginning of these words:

jade **j**oke **j**ump **j**ust **w**ater **w**ild **w**ish **w**oke **y**ak **y**ear **y**es **y**our

A. Write letters to form the words above. Then read each word out loud.

j — — —   y — —   w — — —   j — — —

y — —   j — — —   w — — — —   w — — —

w — — —   y — — —   y — — —   j — — —

B. Write four words that begin with each sound. Use the words you formed above. Then add your own words to the last two rows.

/j/ sound	/w/ sound	/y/ sound

Practice It!
consonant sounds
/j/, /w/, /y/

Answer These Riddles!

A. Read each word out loud. Listen for the sound of /j/, /w/, or /y/ at the beginning. Circle the letter that stands for the sound.

> jade   yell   joke   wings
>
> yellow   walrus   yard   jumping

B. Use the words above to answer the riddles.

1. You laugh at me, but my feelings aren't hurt. _____
2. I have three feet. _____
3. I am a stone and a color. _____
4. Most bugs have four of these. _____
5. Some of my teeth grow outside of my lips. _____
6. I am a way a frog can spend its day. _____
7. My light is between red and green. _____
8. I am not quiet. _____

C. Write a riddle for the word *yesterday*.

_____

_____

Name _____

Sounds of /kw/, /ks/, and /z/

The letters **q**, **x**, and **z** are consonants.

The consonant **q** is almost always followed by **u**. The letters **qu** usually stand for the **/kw/** sound. Listen for the **/kw/** sound at the beginning of these words:

queen   **qu**estion   **qu**ick   **qu**ite

The consonant **x** often stands for the **/ks/** sound. Listen for the **/ks/** sound at the end of these words:

a**x**   bo**x**   fi**x**   mi**x**

The consonant **z** usually stands for the **/z/** sound. Listen for the **/z/** sound at the beginning or end.

zebra   **z**ero   fro**z**e   si**z**e

A. Write letters to form the words above. Then read each word out loud.

/kw/ spelled *qu*	/ks/ spelled *x*	/z/ spelled *z*
q u __ __ __	__ x	__ __ z __
q u __ __ __	__ __ x	z __ __ __
q u __ __ __	__ __ x	z __ __ __ __
q u __ __ __ __ __ __	__ __ x	__ __ __ z __

B. Fill in the chart with words from above or with your own words.

Begins with the /kw/ sound	Ends with the /ks/ sound	Begins or ends with the /z/ sound

Practice It!
consonant sounds
/kw/, /ks/, /z/

Name _____

Find Those Words!

A. Read each word out loud. Write it in the row to show what sound you hear.

> quilt   fixed   zone   quick   boxer   size   zebra   quit   mix

/ks/ spelled *x*			
/z/ spelled *z*			
/kw/ spelled *qu*			

B. Circle the words above in the puzzle. The words can read down, across, or diagonally.

```
Z I M S Q S Z B R N K
E Z O N Q I S X A C C
B Z X A U Z D T I X C
U O X F I E L U E I E
Q N D U T I Q B F S C
F E Q O U X B O X E R
I Z X Q B F X X E Q N
F I X E D E Z E B R A
E X Z X M I X E D I R
```

C. Write the circled words on the lines.

_____   _____   _____

_____   _____   _____

_____   _____   _____

Review It!

consonant sounds
/kw/, /ks/, /z/

Name _____

Fill in the circle by the word that best completes each sentence.

Jack and Wendy

1. Jack and Wendy _____ into the car with their mom and dad.

    Ⓐ waxed Ⓑ mixed Ⓒ jumped

2. They were heading to the _____ to see the wild animals.

    Ⓐ zoo Ⓑ farm Ⓒ west

3. "We have a pony with us," _____ Dad as he gave Wendy's ponytail a tug.

    Ⓐ wished Ⓑ joked Ⓒ fixed

4. Mom said, "Let's _____ get in line to see the seals."

    Ⓐ quite Ⓑ queen Ⓒ quickly

5. "Wow! That walrus is huge!" Jack said. "It spends most of its life in _____."

    Ⓐ water Ⓑ snow Ⓒ rocks

6. "You know, _____ sea lions are called pups," said Wendy.

    Ⓐ your Ⓑ young Ⓒ quiet

7. "It's great how sea lions can _____ on their flippers!" Jack added.

    Ⓐ freeze Ⓑ yak Ⓒ walk

8. "You two kids are _____ the experts on seals!" Mom said.

    Ⓐ quite Ⓑ quick Ⓒ quit

Name _____

Double Final Consonants

Double consonants usually have the same sound as the single consonant.

| dd sounds like /d/ | ff sounds like /f/ | gg sounds like /g/ |
| a**dd** | hu**ff** | e**gg** |

| ll sounds like /l/ | ss sounds like /s/ | zz sounds like /z/ |
| i**ll** | gla**ss** | bu**zz** |

A. Read each word out loud. Circle the letters that have the sound of /d/, /f/, /g/, /l/, /s/, or /z/ at the end.

odd	egg	puff	stiff
stuff	dull	wall	class
press	toss	fizz	fuzz

B. Follow the directions. Use words from above or add your own words.

1. Write three words that end in **ss**.

   _____   _____   _____

2. Write three words that end in **ll**.

   _____   _____   _____

3. Write one word that ends in **gg** and one word that ends in **dd**.

   _____   _____

4. Write one word that ends in **ff** and one word that ends in **zz**.

   _____   _____

Name _____

Practice It!
consonant sounds
/d/, /f/, /g/, /l/, /s/, /z/

Make the Word!

A. Read each word out loud. Circle the two consonants that have the **/d/**, **/f/**, **/g/**, **/l/**, **/s/**, or **/z/** sound.

> add   egg   fizz   tall
>
> class   huff   across   small

B. Add the letters **dd**, **ff**, **ll**, **ss**, or **zz** to form the word that best completes the sentence. Read the word out loud.

1. Liz got her new dress at the ma___ ___.

2. I cannot find my shoes in this me___ ___!

3. The sme___ ___ from the trash made me hold my nose.

4. Bees bu___ ___ when they move their wings fast.

5. A dog can sni___ ___ out smells that people miss.

6. I need to clean out the stu___ ___ in my backpack.

7. It is o___ ___ that zebras do not look the same.

8. Brad gave a ye___ ___ when his team won the game.

9. A snail has a she___ ___ and one foot.

10. I will add some ice to my gla___ ___ of tea.

Review It!

consonant sounds
/d/, /f/, /l/, /s/, /z/

Name _____

Fill in the circle by the word that best completes each sentence.

A Class Not to Miss!

1. We quickly _____ for PE when the last buzzer goes off.
   - Ⓐ pass
   - Ⓑ class
   - Ⓒ dress

2. PE class is outdoors _____ it rains.
   - Ⓐ fuss
   - Ⓑ unless
   - Ⓒ press

3. Sometimes I feel _____ until I do the warmups.
   - Ⓐ stiff
   - Ⓑ cliff
   - Ⓒ fluff

4. We _____ a ball back and forth.
   - Ⓐ toss
   - Ⓑ boss
   - Ⓒ moss

5. Then we run laps, and I huff and _____ when we're done.
   - Ⓐ fluff
   - Ⓑ puff
   - Ⓒ stuff

6. The kids in my _____ like to play baseball the most.
   - Ⓐ grass
   - Ⓑ glass
   - Ⓒ class

7. Judd once hit the _____ through a glass window.
   - Ⓐ call
   - Ⓑ bell
   - Ⓒ ball

8. That ball took _____ like a rocket!
   - Ⓐ off
   - Ⓑ staff
   - Ⓒ puff

And the Answer Is...

Jess saw her hand shake. Water in her glass spilled onto her dress. "What did I get myself into?" she thought.

Mr. Wilson had called Jess yesterday. "Jade is ill with the flu," he said. "We need three players to be on *Quiz Kids*. You're one of the smartest kids in the class. Please join the team."

Jess jumped as yellow lights flashed. The game was about to begin. Bill Jones, the host, said, "Welcome to *Quiz Kids*! Two teams will play today for the grand prize. Alex, Jess, and Zack are from E. B. White School. Judd, Yasmin, and Zoe are from Jane Yolen Middle School."

Mr. Jones told the rules. He would ask a question. The first team to buzz would get to answer. If the answer was wrong, the other team would get to try.

"Let's begin," said Jones. "What is the name for a wild ox with shaggy hair?"

Alex scored when he said, "Yak."

The questions and answers came quickly. Jess just stood there. "In what game does a player trap a king? Chess. How long does it take the Earth to orbit the sun? A year. What animal has black and white stripes? Zebra. What animal has tusks and short stiff hair and…"

Jess buzzed at last. She shouted, "Elephant!"

"No. Team Yolen, what animal has tusks and short stiff hair and lives in the sea?"

Yasmin answered, "Walrus."

"That's correct," said Mr. Jones. "We've got ourselves a tie. Here's the last question. What is the word *flu* short for?"

Judd reached for the buzzer, but Jess hit first. "Influenza," she said.

"Yes! Team White wins!"

Jess gave a yell. She still felt shaky, but in a good way.

Apply It!
consonant sounds

Name _____

Now Try This...

1. Look back at the story. Write a word for each sound.

   /j/_____ /w/_____ /y/_____

   /kw/_____ /z/_____ /ks/_____

2. Write words from the story that have double consonants with these sounds:

   /d/_____ /f/_____ /s/_____

   /z/_____ /l/_____

3. Why might kids want to be on *Quiz Kids?*

   _____
   _____

4. Why do you think Jess didn't answer any questions for most of the quiz?

   _____
   _____

5. What could be a reason Jess knew the answer to the last question?

   _____
   _____

6. Practice reading the first three paragraphs in the story. Then read them to your teacher.

Long and Short Vowel Sounds and Patterns

a, e, i, o, u, y

Overview
The **Long and Short Vowel Sounds and Patterns** section has two purposes: 1) to help students read long and short vowel sounds in words with the most common spellings of the sounds; and 2) to help students analyze words for letter patterns (CVC, CVCC, CVCe) and determine how the pattern affects the word's pronunciation.

Teaching Tips
You may want to use the following techniques to introduce the concepts in this section:

Letter/Sound Relationships *pages 40–74*
Model for students the strategy of blending sounds to say a word. Without pausing, string together the sounds of the consonants and vowels as they appear in a word. Point to each sound and stretch the sound as you say it. End by pronouncing the word as a word. For each "Learn It!" page, have students blend the listed words out loud in the same way you modeled.

Short and Long Vowel Sounds *pages 40–62*
Students will work with words having short and long vowel sounds, including word pairs where the addition of a silent *e* turns a short vowel sound into a long vowel sound. Write the following words on the board, and then ask students to read them out loud:

at, fin, mop, cub

Invite volunteers to add an *e* at the end of each word. Ask students to say the new words. Then have students read each word by covering and then uncovering the *e.*

Vowel Patterns *pages 64–74*
Before students work with determining CVC, CVCC, and CVCe patterns, you may wish to review vowels and consonants by writing the alphabet on the board. Have students write a large letter **C** on one side of a sheet of paper and a large **V** on the other side. As you point to each letter of the alphabet, have students hold up the side of the paper that identifies the letter as a consonant or a vowel. Write either **C** or **V** on the board as each letter is identified.

Rule Breakers
In the **Consonant Sounds** section, the *y* was seen as a consonant. In this section, students learn the function of *y* as a vowel. Help students see that when *y* comes at the end of a syllable or a word, it often has the sound of *i*, as in *cry,* or *e*, as in *jolly.*

Pretest

vowel sounds
short and long *a*, *e*, *i*

Name _____

Read the first word in each row out loud. Fill in the circle by the word that has the same vowel sound.

1. bat	Ⓐ plan	Ⓑ plane	Ⓒ rate	Ⓓ cage
2. make	Ⓐ Sam	Ⓑ rabbit	Ⓒ black	Ⓓ same
3. rest	Ⓐ cake	Ⓑ bent	Ⓒ reed	Ⓓ teen
4. me	Ⓐ her	Ⓑ deck	Ⓒ these	Ⓓ sent
5. skip	Ⓐ kind	Ⓑ fish	Ⓒ fine	Ⓓ stripe
6. slide	Ⓐ dime	Ⓑ dim	Ⓒ drip	Ⓓ skin
7. feed	Ⓐ home	Ⓑ web	Ⓒ being	Ⓓ help
8. trip	Ⓐ hike	Ⓑ find	Ⓒ dime	Ⓓ lift

Long and Short Vowel Sounds and Patterns

Phonics

Learn It!
vowel sounds

Name _____

The Short *a* Sound and Long *a* Sound

Vowels are letters. **a e i o u**

Each vowel can stand for a short sound or a long sound.

Listen for the **short *a*** sound or the **long *a*** sound in the words below.

Short *a*	Long *a*
t**a**p	t**a**pe
h**a**nd	g**a**me
ant	sp**a**ce

A. Read each word out loud. Write **S** above each letter **a** that has the **short a** sound. Write **L** above each letter **a** that has the **long a** sound.

$\overset{S}{\text{S}}$am   same   fake   stand

fade   black   brand   last

plan   plane   plate   trade

B. Write three words that have the **short a** sound and three words that have the **long a** sound. Use the words above. Then add your own words to the last three rows.

Short *a*	Long *a*

Long and Short Vowel Sounds and Patterns

Practice It!
vowel sounds
short and long *a*

Name _____

Animal Clues

A. Read each word out loud. Write **S** above each letter *a* that has the **short a** sound. Write **L** above each letter *a* that has the **long a** sound.

> rabbit   snakes   plan   cage
>
> cape   cap   plane   tame

B. Write a word from above to answer each clue.

1. A lion cannot fit this on his mane.   _____

2. These animals don't have legs.   _____

3. A flying bat seems to have one of these.   _____

4. This animal can jump 12 feet.   _____

5. This is a good home for a hamster.   _____

6. This is a good thing to do before getting a pet.   _____

7. This is a word for animals that are not wild.   _____

8. This is shaped like a bird.   _____

C. Write a clue about an animal using the word *mask*.

_____

_____

Review It!

vowel sounds
short and long *a*

Name _____

Fill in the circle by the word that best completes each sentence.

Plans for a Plane

1. Sam wanted to make a small _____ to hang over his bed.
   - Ⓐ plan
   - Ⓑ plane
   - Ⓒ place

2. "I'll help," said Sam's brother, Jake. "First, you'll need some _____."
   - Ⓐ pages
   - Ⓑ planes
   - Ⓒ plans

3. "Dad said the _____ thing," Sam said. "We got a kit."
   - Ⓐ Sam
   - Ⓑ same
   - Ⓒ shape

4. "I'm making a jet and painting it _____ with gold marks," Sam went on.
   - Ⓐ blame
   - Ⓑ blast
   - Ⓒ black

5. Jake said, "Well, I sure made a mess the _____ time I worked on a plane."
   - Ⓐ last
   - Ⓑ late
   - Ⓒ lake

6. "Let's make a dropcloth out of this old _____," Sam said.
   - Ⓐ sleep
   - Ⓑ sheet
   - Ⓒ steep

7. "We can _____ the sheet to the floor," Sam told Jake.
   - Ⓐ tape
   - Ⓑ tap
   - Ⓒ tame

8. "Mom will be _____ if you don't make a mess," Jake said.
   - Ⓐ glad
   - Ⓑ grab
   - Ⓒ grand

Long and Short Vowel Sounds and Patterns
Phonics

Learn It!
vowel sounds

Name _____

The Short e Sound and Long e Sound

The vowel **e** can stand for the **short e** sound or the **long e** sound.

Listen for the **short e** sound or the **long e** sound in the words below.

Short e	Long e
sh**e**d	f**ee**
r**e**st	b**e**ing
end	sw**ee**t

A. Read each word out loud. Write **S** above each letter **e** that has the **short e** sound. Write **L** above each letter **e** that has the **long e** sound.

b\u0065nt (S)   chess   teeth   sent

fed   feed   bled   bleed

sleep   maybe   pet   three

B. Write three words that have the **short e** sound and three words that have the **long e** sound. Use the words above. Then add your own words to the last three rows.

Short e	Long e

Long and Short Vowel Sounds and Patterns

Practice It!

vowel sounds
short and long **e**

Name _____

Rhyme Time!

A. Read each word out loud. Write **S** above each letter **e** that has the **short e** sound. Write **L** above each letter **e** that has the **long e** sound.

> queen   sheep   bed   sleep
>
> sent   cent   tent   shed

B. Choose words from above to complete the rhyme.

Bree said it was time that she _____

a list of the many ways that she spent

so many dollars and every last _____

on one sleeping bag and a little green _____.

"I want to go camping, but not in a _____.

I'll sleep on the grass with a soft bag as my _____.

If I can't get to _____,

I'll try counting _____."

Bree was last seen

camped out like a _____.

C. Write a **long e** word to complete the rhyme.

I do not think I have ever seen

a patch of grass that shade of _____!

Review It!

vowel sounds
short and long **e**

Name _____

Fill in the circle by the word that best completes each sentence.

The Sheep Vet

1. Dr. Steen is a _____ who cares for sheep.

    Ⓐ pet   Ⓑ vet   Ⓒ net

2. She looks after different _____, or kinds, of sheep.

    Ⓐ breads   Ⓑ bleeds   Ⓒ breeds

3. Dr. Steen checks the sheep's _____ to see if they are well.

    Ⓐ keep   Ⓑ teeth   Ⓒ sleep

4. She makes sure a sheep is not sick with a _____.

    Ⓐ sheet   Ⓑ rest   Ⓒ fever

5. She knows that sheep _____ good when they are fed the right food.

    Ⓐ feel   Ⓑ fed   Ⓒ bled

6. The vet tells farmers to keep _____ away from their sheep.

    Ⓐ press   Ⓑ pests   Ⓒ nests

7. Dr. Steen _____ long hours checking sheep.

    Ⓐ feels   Ⓑ frees   Ⓒ spends

8. Sometimes she hardly _____ when she is on call.

    Ⓐ sleeps   Ⓑ meets   Ⓒ seeds

Name _____

Learn It!
vowel sounds

The Short *i* Sound and Long *i* Sound

The vowel *i* can stand for the **short *i*** sound or the **long *i*** sound.

Listen for the **short *i*** sound or the **long *i*** sound in the words below.

Short *i*	Long *i*
itch	ice
rib	lime
begin	spider

A. Read each word out loud. Write **S** above each letter *i* that has the **short *i*** sound. Write **L** above each letter *i* that has the **long *i*** sound.

<small>S</small>
rip   ripe   drip   skin

still   mist   grind   spice

dim   dime   line   mile

B. Write three words that have the **short *i*** sound and three words that have the **long *i*** sound. Use the words above. Then add your own words to the last three rows.

Short *i*	Long *i*

Long and Short Vowel Sounds and Patterns
Phonics

Practice It!

vowel sounds
short and long *i*

Name _____

One Way...

A. Read each word out loud. Write **S** above each letter *i* that has the **short i** sound. Write **L** above each letter *i* that has the **long i** sound.

smile	ship	fish	dim	slide
dime	swim	rip	bike	skip

B. Draw lines to match the clues to the words.

1. one way to get through the woods   a. fish

2. one way to send things   b. hike

3. one way to show you are happy   c. slide

4. one way to make paper strips   d. ship

5. one way to move a ball   e. swim

6. one way to get your food   f. kick

7. one way to play on ice   g. smile

8. one way to play in water   h. rip

C. Write a "one way" clue for the word *bike*.

one way _____

_____

Review It!

vowel sounds
short and long *i*

Name _____

Fill in the circle by the word that best completes each sentence.

Time to Smile

1. Justin was having a boring day, and it was _____ for a change.
   - Ⓐ tire
   - Ⓑ time
   - Ⓒ tide

2. He made a _____ of the things he liked to do.
   - Ⓐ list
   - Ⓑ line
   - Ⓒ lift

3. Riding his _____ around the lake was at the top of his list.
   - Ⓐ bite
   - Ⓑ kite
   - Ⓒ bike

4. "I wonder if Dad _____ taking a short drive," Justin thought.
   - Ⓐ minds
   - Ⓑ kinds
   - Ⓒ limes

5. Dad said a drive was fine. "I'll _____ while you bike," said Dad.
   - Ⓐ hide
   - Ⓑ hive
   - Ⓒ hike

6. "We can take our _____ lines, too," said Justin.
   - Ⓐ wishing
   - Ⓑ fishing
   - Ⓒ filling

7. "I put some _____ melon slices in the cooler," Dad said.
   - Ⓐ rip
   - Ⓑ ripe
   - Ⓒ ride

8. "Let's head out!" Justin said as he gave his dad a big _____.
   - Ⓐ slip
   - Ⓑ slide
   - Ⓒ smile

Long and Short Vowel Sounds and Patterns
Phonics

Read It!
vowel sounds

Amber Gets a Pet

"No, not yet." That's the answer Amber always got. For years she had asked her parents for a pet. This year they gave in.

Amber and her sister Meg went to an animal shelter. Amber quickly fell in love with a black cat named Wilma.

"Mom won't like a cat," said Meg. "A cat would shred her new chairs."

So Amber looked at the dogs. She knew that a dog had to be walked every day. That would be hard when it was cold outside.

Amber bent down and looked into a rabbit cage. A white rabbit sat and twitched its whiskers. Amber asked, "What do rabbits like to do?"

Meg said, "They dig and chew. They need to chew to keep their teeth from growing too long. Rabbits can chew through wires and wood."

Amber could picture the rabbit chewing the legs off the new chairs. Mom and Dad would be so mad! Maybe a different pet would be better.

A snake could be fun. It would be neat to see it shed its skin. But, it would be gross to feed it mice. Fish were quiet, but they couldn't be held.

Then Amber saw a lizard in a tank. The lizard rested on a small branch. A heat lamp warmed its skin. All it ate were greens and bugs. This pet would not shred chairs or need a walk.

"What's that spray bottle for?" Amber asked a worker.

"The tank can't get dry. We mist the tank with water. Are you interested in a lizard?"

"I'll come back with my mom and dad," Amber said. She smiled as she planned what to tell them.

Long and Short Vowel Sounds and Patterns

Apply It!
vowel sounds

Name _____

Now Try This...

1. Look back at the paragraph where Amber sees the lizard. Write two words for each sound.

Short *a* (as in *cat*) spelled *a*	Long *a* spelled *a*	Short *e* spelled *e*

Long *e* spelled *ee*	Short *i* spelled *i*

2. What could be a reason why Amber's parents did not let her have a pet?

   _____

   _____

3. Why didn't Amber want a rabbit?

   _____

   _____

4. How could Amber talk her parents into letting her have a lizard?

   _____

   _____

5. Practice reading two paragraphs in the story. Then read them to your teacher.

Pretest

vowel sounds
short and long **o, u, y**

Name _____

A. Fill in the circle by the word that has the same vowel sound as the first word in the row.

1. pond	Ⓐ cone	Ⓑ wove	Ⓒ hero	Ⓓ drop
2. poke	Ⓐ open	Ⓑ frog	Ⓒ clock	Ⓓ plot
3. drum	Ⓐ cube	Ⓑ blue	Ⓒ brush	Ⓓ huge
4. tune	Ⓐ trunk	Ⓑ truth	Ⓒ tusk	Ⓓ tub
5. dust	Ⓐ plum	Ⓑ cute	Ⓒ unit	Ⓓ due

B. Fill in the circle by the word with the same sound of *y* as the first word in the row.

1. dry	Ⓐ sunny	Ⓑ party	Ⓒ funny	Ⓓ spy
2. pony	Ⓐ try	Ⓑ fry	Ⓒ happy	Ⓓ dye
3. windy	Ⓐ type	Ⓑ shy	Ⓒ silly	Ⓓ cry

Long and Short Vowel Sounds and Patterns

Learn It!
vowel sounds

Name _____

The Short *o* Sound and Long *o* Sound

The vowel **o** can stand for the **short o** sound or the **long o** sound.

Listen for the **short o** sound or the **long o** sound in the words below.

Short *o*	Long *o*
odd	**o**mit
m**o**p	m**o**pe
bl**o**ck	her**o**

A. Read each word out loud. Write **S** above each letter **o** that has the **short o** sound. Write **L** above each letter **o** that has the **long o** sound.

      L
broke   dock   alone   clothes

pond   rock   code   shop

shock   globe   plot   zero

B. Write three words that have the **short o** sound and three words that have the **long o** sound. Use the words above. Then add your own words to the last three rows.

Short *o*	Long *o*

Long and Short Vowel Sounds and Patterns

Phonics

Practice It!
vowel sounds
short and long **o**

Name _____

What's the Word?

A. Read each word out loud. Write **S** above each letter **o** that has the **short o** sound. Write **L** above each letter **o** that has the **long o** sound.

> crops   broken   mop   shock   hero
>
> omit   mope   robe   pond   smoke

B. Choose words from above that go with the definitions.

1. to wash the floor   ___ ___ ___
2. in pieces; not working   ___ ___ ___ ___ ___ ___
3. to be sad   ___ ___ ___ ___
4. a brave or good person   ___ ___ ___ ___
5. plants often used for food   ___ ___ ___ ___ ___
6. to leave something out   ___ ___ ___ ___
7. a small body of still water   ___ ___ ___ ___
8. what is given off when something burns   ___ ___ ___ ___ ___

C. Write a definition for the word *home*.

_____

_____

Long and Short Vowel Sounds and Patterns

Review It!

vowel sounds
short and long **o**

Name _____

Fill in the circle by the word that best completes each sentence.

Time to Shop

1. Hope liked to _____ with her mom.

    Ⓐ chop   Ⓑ drop   Ⓒ shop

2. Today, Hope shopped _____.

    Ⓐ omit   Ⓑ alone   Ⓒ broke

3. Hope needed some new _____ for school.

    Ⓐ clocks   Ⓑ clothes   Ⓒ closes

4. She also wanted to make a _____ for her mom.

    Ⓐ rob   Ⓑ rope   Ⓒ robe

5. Hope looked at cloth and liked the _____ cloth most.

    Ⓐ cotton   Ⓑ bottom   Ⓒ clock

6. She picked cloth that was the color of a red _____.

    Ⓐ fog   Ⓑ ox   Ⓒ fox

7. Hope got the cloth, and she got some _____ buttons, too.

    Ⓐ gold   Ⓑ code   Ⓒ sold

8. "Mom will be _____ when she sees what I made her!" said Hope.

    Ⓐ flocked   Ⓑ locked   Ⓒ shocked

Name _____

Learn It!
vowel sounds

The Short *u* Sound and Long *u* Sound

The vowel *u* can stand for the **short *u*** sound or the **long *u*** sound.

Listen for the **short *u*** sound or the **long *u*** sound in the words below.

Short *u*	Long *u*
upon	**u**nit
t**u**b	t**u**be
br**u**sh	men**u**

A. Read each word out loud. Write **S** above each letter *u* that has the **short *u*** sound. Write **L** above each letter *u* that has the **long *u*** sound.

    S
cub   cube   gum   blue

hug   huge   flute   upset

menu   dust   clump   usual

B. Write three words that have the **short *u*** sound and three words that have the **long *u*** sound. Use the words above. Then add your own words to the last three rows.

Short *u*	Long *u*

Long and Short Vowel Sounds and Patterns

Phonics

Practice It!

vowel sounds
short and long **u**

Name _____

One Way...

A. Read each word out loud. Write **S** above each letter **u** that has the **short u** sound. Write **L** above each letter **u** that has the **long u** sound.

> dunk   dust   fume   brush   bump
>
> cut   hug   Luke   tube   unless

B. Draw lines to match the clues to the words.

1. one way to make paper strips   a. bump

2. one way to get the ball in the basket   b. Luke

3. one way to show you care   c. fume

4. one way to show you are mad   d. cut

5. one way to fix your hair   e. brush

6. one way to push   f. hug

7. one way to name a boy   g. dust

8. one way to clean   h. dunk

C. Choose a **long u** word and a **short u** word from the box above. Write a clue for each word.

_____

_____

_____

Long and Short Vowel Sounds and Patterns

Review It!

vowel sounds
short and long **u**

Name _____

Fill in the circle by the word that best completes each sentence.

Aunt June and Chuck

1. Chuck gets uneasy as his aunt and uncle drive up in their _____.

   Ⓐ trunk   Ⓑ truck   Ⓒ tuck

2. Chuck knows what is coming, so he tries to _____.

   Ⓐ huge   Ⓑ dunk   Ⓒ duck

3. "Chuckie!" yells Aunt June as she _____ in the door.

   Ⓐ hushes   Ⓑ rushes   Ⓒ mushes

4. Aunt June throws her arms around Chuck and gives him _____.

   Ⓐ huge   Ⓑ hugs   Ⓒ rugs

5. Chuck's aunt makes him _____ when she calls him "Chuckie."

   Ⓐ blush   Ⓑ brush   Ⓒ duck

6. She hasn't a _____ what makes Chuck turn red.

   Ⓐ cube   Ⓑ cute   Ⓒ clue

7. Aunt June _____ calls him Chuckie all day long.

   Ⓐ usual   Ⓑ usually   Ⓒ unless

8. The _____ is, Chuck is okay with the hugs, but he hates the nickname.

   Ⓐ trust   Ⓑ truth   Ⓒ trunk

Name _____

The Sounds of y

The letter **y** can have the **long e** or the **long i** vowel sounds.

Listen for the sounds of **y** in the words below.

Long e Sound	Long i Sound
plent**y**	dr**y**
happ**y**	sl**y**
an**y**thing	cr**y**ing

A. Read each word out loud. Write **E** above the letter **y** when it has the **long e** sound. Write **I** above the letter **y** when it has the **long i** sound.

    E
sill**y**   sh**y**   dr**y**   mudd**y**

an**y**one   bod**y**   sunn**y**   cand**y**

tr**y**   t**y**pe   repl**y**   sp**y**

B. Fill in the first three rows of the chart. Use six of the words above. Then add your own words to the last three rows.

y has the long *e* sound	*y* has the long *i* sound

Practice It!
vowel sounds
sounds of y

Name _____

Crossword Time!

A. Read the words out loud. Write **E** above the letter **y** when it has the **long e** sound. Write **I** above the letter **y** when it has the **long i** sound.

| puppy | fly | anytime | muddy | why |
| body | silly | bury | shy | happy |

B. Use the words above to complete the crossword puzzle.

Down

1. a bug with two wings
2. feeling joy
4. covered with mud
6. bashful
7. to hide in the ground

Across

3. whenever
5. all the parts of you
6. foolish
8. a young dog
9. a question word

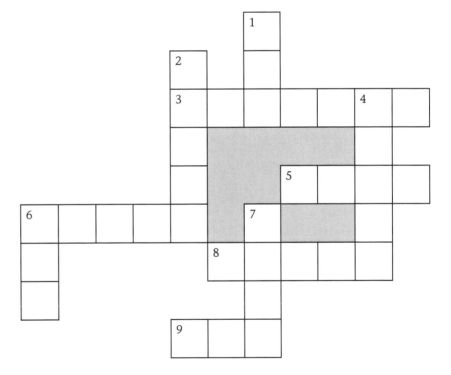

Long and Short Vowel Sounds and Patterns

Phonics 59

Review It!

vowel sounds
sounds of **y**

Name _____

Fill in the circle by the word that best completes each sentence.

A Wet Party

1. July was really hot, so I wanted to have a swim _____.

    Ⓐ pretty   Ⓑ party   Ⓒ plenty

2. My _____ said I could invite ten friends.

    Ⓐ family   Ⓑ country   Ⓒ silly

3. I told Mom that I would get the food ready by _____.

    Ⓐ my   Ⓑ myself   Ⓒ lady

4. I made _____ of dips to go with the bags of chips.

    Ⓐ many   Ⓑ really   Ⓒ plenty

5. Dad helped me _____ the cover off the pool.

    Ⓐ buy   Ⓑ fry   Ⓒ pry

6. The sky was clear and _____ when the party began.

    Ⓐ sunny   Ⓑ sticky   Ⓒ lucky

7. But then it turned _____, and we got muddy as we ran back to the house.

    Ⓐ pretty   Ⓑ rainy   Ⓒ funny

8. Mom gave us towels so we could _____ off before going inside.

    Ⓐ dry   Ⓑ shy   Ⓒ spy

Read It!
vowel sounds

BOGS FULL OF CLUES

Some of the best clues about life in the past are found in mud. Bogs are filled with things buried long ago.

Bogs are small wetlands. Plants grow in bogs. The ground is wet so the plants tend to rot. When they rot, they form peat. Germs do not grow in peat. Things that were buried in peat long ago stay in good shape.

In 1950, a family in Denmark was shocked to spy a body in a bog. The body did not look old. But scientists said the person had lived around 2,000 years ago! The bog had turned the body into a mummy. Scientists call the body the Tollund Man (**Tol**-lund) because he was found near the village of Tollund.

Clothes have been dug up in bogs, too. Many of the clothes found in bogs in Denmark date back to the same time as the Tollund Man.

People at that time wore clothes made from the skins of ox and sheep. Women wove their dresses, too. One style of dress looked like a tube. Pins were used to close the tube dress at the top. Most people wore fur capes. They also wore leg warmers made of sheep's wool. Clothing of bright colors have been found in bogs in Denmark. People used the plants that grew in the area to dye their cloth.

Wet, muddy bogs also hold objects used at the time of the Tollund Man. Bones made into tools have been found. Some bones were used to hunt ducks and wildlife. Pots have been found, too. They were used to store and cook food. Clues show that people ate nuts, berries, and meat.

Next time you see a wetland, or bog, think about the clues you would bury. What would they tell about you?

Apply It!
vowel sounds

Name _____

Now Try This...

1. Look back at the story. Write three words for each sound.

short *o*	long *o*	short *u*	long *u*	*y* with the long *e* sound

2. Leg warmers and fur capes have been found in bogs. What do the objects tell you about the weather of the area?

   _____

3. Name three ways that people today are like the people who lived 2,000 years ago in Denmark.

   _____

   _____

   _____

4. List an item that could be buried in a bog today. Explain what that item tells about life in today's world.

   _____

   _____

   _____

5. Practice reading a long paragraph in the story. Then read it to your teacher.

Pretest
vowel patterns
CVC, CVCC, CVCe

Name _____

A. Fill in the circle next to the word in each row that has the short vowel sound in the middle (CVC).

1. Ⓐ add Ⓑ hum Ⓒ ice
2. Ⓐ ace Ⓑ ask Ⓒ nap
3. Ⓐ hop Ⓑ end Ⓒ odd
4. Ⓐ ate Ⓑ she Ⓒ sub

B. Fill in the circle next to the word in each row that has the short vowel sound followed by consonants (CVCC).

1. Ⓐ pane Ⓑ hand Ⓒ tile
2. Ⓐ bent Ⓑ boot Ⓒ line
3. Ⓐ heel Ⓑ soft Ⓒ dome

C. Fill in the circle next to the word in each row that has the long vowel sound (CVCe).

1. Ⓐ tune Ⓑ trip Ⓒ slip
2. Ⓐ ramp Ⓑ lime Ⓒ lids
3. Ⓐ toss Ⓑ tops Ⓒ tone
4. Ⓐ risk Ⓑ rate Ⓒ rats

Long and Short Vowel Sounds and Patterns

Name _____

The CVC Pattern

The order in which letters appear in a word can help you figure out how to say the word. Words that have the consonant-vowel-consonant pattern (CVC) usually have a short vowel sound.

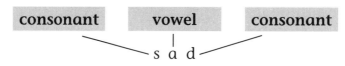

A. Read each word out loud. Circle the vowel. Then draw a line to the vowel sound you hear.

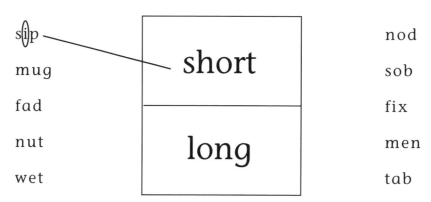

sip — short

mug

fad

nut

long

wet

nod

sob

fix

men

tab

B. Look at the lines you made above. Write the word that makes the sentence true.

I have learned that the vowel sound between two consonants

usually is _____.
(short, long)

C. Add letters to make your own CVC words for each vowel sound.

CVC Short *a*	CVC Short *e*	CVC Short *i*	CVC Short *o*	CVC Short *u*
__a__	__e__	__i__	__o__	__u__
__a__	__e__	__i__	__o__	__u__

Long and Short Vowel Sounds and Patterns

Practice It!
vowel patterns
CVC

Name _____

What Am I?

A. Read each word out loud. Write **C** above each consonant. Write **V** above each short vowel sound.

> CVC
> dab   rot   sob   hip   hem
> lug   map   tin   net   cut

B. Write the missing vowel to spell the word that goes with the clue. Read the word out loud.

1. I am a dog with a flat nose.   p ___ g

2. I am a car you pay to use.   c ___ b

3. I am a way to close a coat.   z ___ p

4. I am a young goat.   k ___ d

5. I am the home of a lion.   d ___ n

6. I am a shell for peas.   p ___ d

7. I am a way to sing.   h ___ m

8. I am a part of a tree that has been cut down.   l ___ g

C. Write an "I am" clue for the word *map*.

I am _____

_____.

Long and Short Vowel Sounds and Patterns
Phonics

Review It!

vowel patterns
CVC

Name _____

Fill in the circle by the word that best completes each sentence.

A Pug for a Pet

1. "Now that I'm _____, I can take care of a pet," Nat said to his mom.

    Ⓐ tan   Ⓑ tin   Ⓒ ten

2. Mom said yes and let Nat pick out a _____.

    Ⓐ pup   Ⓑ put   Ⓒ pat

3. Nat came home from the pet shop holding a black _____.

    Ⓐ dug   Ⓑ rug   Ⓒ pug

4. Nat named her _____ because that's the sound she made when she barked.

    Ⓐ Pup   Ⓑ Yip   Ⓒ Ken

5. He put a blanket in a _____ to make the dog a bed.

    Ⓐ box   Ⓑ mix   Ⓒ pan

6. But Yip began to _____ the blanket across the floor.

    Ⓐ dip   Ⓑ lug   Ⓒ tip

7. Then she played a fast game of _____ with Nat.

    Ⓐ tag   Ⓑ lag   Ⓒ rut

8. "Now she's ready for a _____," Nat said as the dog got in her box.

    Ⓐ cap   Ⓑ hat   Ⓒ nap

Learn It!
vowel patterns

Name _____

The CVCC Pattern

Look at the pattern CVCC. See how CVCC differs from CVC.
Two consonants follow the vowel in the CVCC pattern.
Like the CVC pattern, CVCC words usually have a short vowel sound.

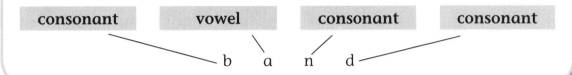

A. For each word, write **C** above the consonants and **V** above the vowel.

CVCC
dent   hand   lump   mask

bond   left   just   soft

lift   miss   lint   sent

B. Read the words above out loud. Then read the sentence below.
Write the word that makes the sentence true.

I have learned that the vowel sound in a consonant-vowel-consonant-consonant

word usually has a _____ sound.
(short, long)

C. Add letters to make your own CVCC words for each vowel sound.

CVCC Short *a*	CVCC Short *e*	CVCC Short *i*	CVCC Short *o*	CVCC Short *u*
__ a __ __	__ e __ __	__ i __ __	__ o __ __	__ u __ __
__ a __ __	__ e __ __	__ i __ __	__ o __ __	__ u __ __

Long and Short Vowel Sounds and Patterns

Practice It!

vowel patterns
CVCC

Name _____

Word Scramble

A. Read each word out loud. Write **C** above each consonant. Write **V** above the vowel.

> gift   send   lung   fond
>
> task   belt   bent   rust

B. Read each clue about dogs. The answer is a CVCC word. Unscramble the answer, and write the missing letters on the lines.

1. what a dog can shake — dnha — __ a __
2. a wild animal in the dog family — fwlo — __ o __
3. how a dog gets what it wants — gbes — __ e __
4. what a dog likes to do to your face — klci — (i) __
5. dogs do this to keep cool — ntap — __ a __
6. a dog of mixed breeds — ttmu — __ u __
7. dogs do this with a lick — siks — __ i __
8. what a dog can be trained to do — elhp — __ e __

C. Unscramble the circled letters above to answer the clue.

You can do this for someone's birthday.

I can __ __ __ __ a __ __ __ __ .

Review It!
vowel patterns
CVCC

Name _____

Fill in the circle by the word that best completes each sentence.

Kent's Gift

1. Kent's dad gave him the best _____ for his birthday!
   - Ⓐ lift
   - Ⓑ golf
   - Ⓒ gift

2. Dad got the gift online, so it was _____ by mail.
   - Ⓐ sent
   - Ⓑ send
   - Ⓒ cold

3. Kent gave the box a shake and heard _____ in it.
   - Ⓐ parks
   - Ⓑ perks
   - Ⓒ parts

4. Kent gave a _____ when he pulled back the lid.
   - Ⓐ disk
   - Ⓑ gasp
   - Ⓒ ring

5. Inside the box was the _____ he had wanted!
   - Ⓐ tent
   - Ⓑ lint
   - Ⓒ land

6. "Can I _____ in the yard on Friday?" asked Kent.
   - Ⓐ lift
   - Ⓑ calm
   - Ⓒ camp

7. "Sure," said Dad. "You can't get _____ back there!"
   - Ⓐ last
   - Ⓑ lost
   - Ⓒ list

8. "Don't fill the tent with _____," Dad added.
   - Ⓐ just
   - Ⓑ sunk
   - Ⓒ junk

Long and Short Vowel Sounds and Patterns

Name _____

Learn It!
vowel patterns

The CVCe Pattern

Words that have the consonant-vowel-consonant-e pattern (CVCe) end in a silent **e**. CVCe words usually have a long vowel sound.

consonant   vowel   consonant   silent e

r i d e

A. Show the CVCe pattern in each word. Write **C** above the consonants and **V** above the vowel. Cross out the silent **e**.

CVC
wav~~e~~   pole   cute   dive

note   hide   fade   save

cube   cone   time   tale

B. Read the words above out loud. Then read the sentence below. Write the word that makes the sentence true.

I have learned that the vowel sound in a consonant-vowel-consonant-*e* word

is usually _____.
(short, long)

C. Add letters to make your own CVCe words for each vowel sound.

CVCe Long a	CVCe Long i	CVCe Long o	CVCe Long u
__ a __ e	__ i __ e	__ o __ e	__ u __ e
__ a __ e	__ i __ e	__ o __ e	__ u __ e
__ a __ e	__ i __ e	__ o __ e	__ u __ e

Long and Short Vowel Sounds and Patterns
Phonics

Practice It!
vowel patterns
CVCe

Name _____

Crossword Time!

A. Read each word out loud. Show the CVCe pattern.

CVC
nic~~k~~   cube   same   vase

ripe   cave   lake   bone

B. Use the words above to complete the crossword puzzle.

Down

1. a 3-D shape
2. what a dog likes to chew
3. a holder for flowers
5. a large hole in the side of a hill

Across

4. kind
6. alike
7. a body of water
8. ready to eat

Review It!

vowel patterns
CVCe

Name _____

Fill in the circle by the word that best completes each sentence.

Not a Cute Pet

1. Kate named her pet snake _____ because he is long and thin.
    - Ⓐ Hose
    - Ⓑ Rose
    - Ⓒ Pose

2. Hose is kept in a _____ that has a lid.
    - Ⓐ wage
    - Ⓑ cake
    - Ⓒ cage

3. Hose is four feet long in _____.
    - Ⓐ wide
    - Ⓑ wise
    - Ⓒ size

4. The snake feeds on dead _____.
    - Ⓐ pile
    - Ⓑ mice
    - Ⓒ nice

5. Like all snakes, Hose is wild and not _____.
    - Ⓐ lame
    - Ⓑ line
    - Ⓒ tame

6. One day, Hose _____ a push on the lid of his cage, and he got out.
    - Ⓐ game
    - Ⓑ gave
    - Ⓒ hide

7. He made his way under a _____ of papers.
    - Ⓐ pile
    - Ⓑ bite
    - Ⓒ hole

8. It took Kate and her family a long _____ to find Hose.
    - Ⓐ tame
    - Ⓑ time
    - Ⓒ fade

LUKE'S JOB

Mrs. Sorg gave Max and Ben a hug. "Go to bed by nine and be nice to Luke." She asked Luke if he was sure he could cope with the boys.

"You bet! It'll be fun," said Luke. He stood tall to show that he could handle two little kids. This was his first babysitting job. He bent down to pat Gus, the family's pug. Gus growled.

"Bad dog! Don't worry. Gus won't bite," said Mr. Sorg.

Ben and Max waved to their mom and dad. The boys looked cute. "This will be easy money," Luke thought.

The boys began to sob as soon as their parents drove away. Gus began to yip and yap. Luke had to think fast. "Let's play a game. You kids hide while I count to ten. Then I'll find you."

Luke walked into the den. He looked in a big vase and under the rug. A chair seemed to giggle. Luke headed into Max's room. Luke looked in a cap and under a box. The door seemed to gasp. The boys hid over and over. Each time they hid under the chair and behind the door.

Luke could not play one more time. He said, "Let's take Gus for a walk." But Gus sat. Luke had to tug him outside.

"Let's run!" said Ben. Of course, Max followed. "Get back here!" yelled Luke. The boys kept going. Luke tried to bribe them. "I'll give you a treat," he yelled.

The boys got a snack, and then got into the tub. Gus sat near. Ben and Max slapped the water to make waves. Luke got wet. Gus got wet. And he growled.

"Time for bed," said Luke.

"No! Tell us a story," the boys said.

So Luke did. He told the tale of the little red hen. He told it over and over and over. When the Sorgs came home, they found three sleeping boys.

Apply It!
vowel patterns

Name _____

Now Try This...

1. Read each word out loud. Listen for the vowel sound. Write each word in the chart to show its pattern of letters.

> nine   Ben   bent   tug   hid
> tub   game   vase   back   gasp

CVC	CVCC	CVCe

2. Do you think Max and Ben liked Luke? _____

   Use a fact from the story to prove your answer.

   _____

   _____

3. What do you think was the hardest part about Luke's job?

   _____

   _____

4. What is one way Luke got the boys to listen to him?

   _____

   _____

5. Practice reading three paragraphs in the story. Then read them to your teacher.

Long and Short Vowel Sounds and Patterns
Phonics

Phonics and Word Study • EMC 3361 • © Evan-Moor Corp.

Consonant Variants and Digraphs

Overview
The purpose of the **Consonant Variants and Digraphs** section is to help students understand that while most consonants have the same sound wherever they appear, certain consonants have different, or varying, sounds. Some consonants' sounds depend on the letters that follow them.

Teaching Tips
You may want to use the following techniques to introduce the concepts in this section:

Hard and Soft *c* and *g* pages 77–82
Write these categories on the board: Hard C, Soft C, Hard G, Soft G. Invite students to brainstorm words that begin with *c* and *g*, and then list each word in its section. Give prompts, if needed, so that both hard and soft *c* and *g* words are suggested. Then find a pattern in the words having a hard sound (*c* or *g* is usually followed by *a, o,* or *u*) and words with a soft sound (*c* or *g* is usually followed by *e* or *i*).

Sounds of *s* pages 83–87
Have students write a large **S** on one side of a sheet of paper and a large **Z** on the other side. Say each of the following words, and have students hold up the side of the paper that represents the sound the *s* stands for: *wise, boss, cheese, gas* (z, s, z, s). Draw a one-sentence conclusion about the sounds of *s* (the letter *s* can have the /s/ sound or the /z/ sound).

Consonant Digraphs pages 89–96
Write a large **s** on a sticky-backed paper and a large **h** on another. Place the letters on the board with a space between them. Have students sound out each letter. Then move the letters side by side and explain that they now have a new sound: /**sh**/, as in *shark* and *dash*. Have students suggest other words that begin with the /**sh**/ sound. In the same manner, introduce **ch, th, wh**. Then introduce **ph** and **gh** (having the /**f**/ sound, as in *graph, laugh,* and *photo*).

Variant Spellings: the /sh/ Sound pages 101–105
Write these words on the board:

   ship, addition, delicious, fiction, shape

Read the words out loud, and have students listen for the sound that is the same in them (/**sh**/). Lead students to determine the pairs of letters that stand for the /**sh**/ sound in each word (*sh, ti, ci, ti, sh*).

Rule Breakers
The /**sh**/ sound is most frequently represented by the *sh* spelling. Students, however, may notice other spellings for the /**sh**/ sound that do not appear in this section. For example, *sh* can be spelled with *s* (*sure*) and *si* (*mansion*). It is good to guide students to use qualifying words, such as *often, usually,* and *sometimes,* when drawing conclusions about letter/sound relationships. For example: The letters *sh* usually have the /**sh**/ sound.

Pretest
consonant variants
sounds of *c, g, s*

Name _____

Read the first word in the row. Fill in the circle next to the sound of the underlined letter.

1. <u>c</u>ase	Ⓐ /k/	Ⓑ /s/	Ⓒ /kw/
2. fa<u>c</u>e	Ⓐ /f/	Ⓑ /s/	Ⓒ /k/
3. <u>g</u>ame	Ⓐ /g/	Ⓑ /j/	Ⓒ /k/
4. <u>s</u>ing	Ⓐ /ks/	Ⓑ /s/	Ⓒ /z/
5. <u>g</u>em	Ⓐ /g/	Ⓑ /j/	Ⓒ /ks/
6. call<u>s</u>	Ⓐ /s/	Ⓑ /k/	Ⓒ /z/
7. <u>s</u>oft	Ⓐ /z/	Ⓑ /sh/	Ⓒ /s/
8. <u>c</u>ent	Ⓐ /s/	Ⓑ /z/	Ⓒ /k/
9. <u>g</u>iant	Ⓐ /g/	Ⓑ /k/	Ⓒ /j/
10. chee<u>s</u>e	Ⓐ /s/	Ⓑ /z/	Ⓒ /j/
11. son<u>g</u>	Ⓐ /g/	Ⓑ /j/	Ⓒ /c/
12. be<u>c</u>ome	Ⓐ /g/	Ⓑ /k/	Ⓒ /s/

Consonant Variants and Digraphs
Phonics

Learn It!
consonant variants

Name _____

Sounds of c

The consonant **c** can stand for the **hard /k/** sound. The **c** also can stand for the **soft /s/** sound. Listen for the sound of **c** in the words below.

Hard c with the /k/ sound (often heard before *a, o, u*)	Soft c with the /s/ sound (often heard before *e, i*)
be**c**ause	fa**c**e
cob	**c**ity
cut	

A. Read each word out loud. Draw a line to the sound of **c** that you hear.

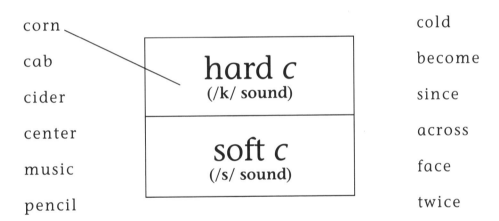

corn
cab
cider
center
music
pencil

cold
become
since
across
face
twice

B. Fill in the chart with your own words. The **c** can be heard at the beginning, middle, or end of a word.

Hard c	Soft c

Practice It!

consonant variants
sounds of c

Name _____

What's the Word?

A. Read the words out loud.
Underline the letter **c** in each word.
Write **k** where you hear the **/k/** sound of **c**.
Write **s** where you hear the **/s/** sound of **c**.

```
      k
   cash        city        corn        office       since

   decide      candy       dance       cupcake      code
```

B. Write a word from above that goes with the clue.

1. a fun way to move to music   ___ ___ ___ ___ ___

2. sweet seeds you can eat   ___ ___ ___ ___

3. a no-no to a dentist   ___ ___ ___ ___ ___

4. to make up your mind   ___ ___ ___ ___ ___ ___

5. what you want to see in your wallet ___ ___ ___ ___

6. a room to work in   ___ ___ ___ ___ ___ ___

7. secret writing   ___ ___ ___ ___

8. a large town where many people live and work   ___ ___ ___ ___

C. Write a clue for the word *circle*.

_____

_____

Review It!

consonant variants
sounds of **c**

Name _____

Fill in the circle by the word that best completes each sentence.

The Camp Race

1. Casey spent two weeks at a summer _____.

    Ⓐ camp   Ⓑ cramp   Ⓒ case

2. On the last day, kids from each _____ held a race.

    Ⓐ cab   Ⓑ cube   Ⓒ cabin

3. The race began at the big cabin called the Kids' _____.

    Ⓐ Nice   Ⓑ Center   Ⓒ Corn

4. The first to reach the dark _____ would be the winner.

    Ⓐ cave   Ⓑ cane   Ⓒ city

5. _____ the day was very hot, the race was less than a mile long.

    Ⓐ Once   Ⓑ Since   Ⓒ Decide

6. Casey tied the _____ on his shoes and felt ready to race.

    Ⓐ codes   Ⓑ paces   Ⓒ laces

7. He ran fast and came in _____ place.

    Ⓐ twice   Ⓑ once   Ⓒ second

8. Then Casey ate cupcakes and drank cold _____ with the other kids.

    Ⓐ rice   Ⓑ cider   Ⓒ cinder

Learn It!
consonant variants

Name _____

Sounds of g

The consonant **g** usually stands for the **hard /g/** sound.
The **g** can stand for the **soft /j/** sound, too.

Listen for the sound of **g** in the words below.

Hard g with the /g/ sound (often heard before *a, o, u*)	Soft g with the /j/ sound (often heard before *e, i*)
be**g**an	ran**g**e
gold	**g**in**g**er
gum	

A. Read each word out loud. Draw a line to the sound you hear.

gave   game
giraffe   flag
cage   **hard g**   wagon
               (/g/ sound)
large   golf
gobble   **soft g**   gem
               (/j/ sound)
gust   magic

B. Fill in the chart with your own words. The **g** can be heard at the beginning, middle, or end of the word.

Hard g	Soft g

Practice It!
consonant variants
sounds of **g**

Name _____

Get a Clue!

A. Read the words out loud.
Underline the letter **g** in each word.
Write **j** where you hear the **/j/** sound.
Write **g** where you hear the **/g/** sound.

j				
giraffe	goldfish	gate	giant	garden
began	gap	page	gulf	gentle

B. Read each clue. Then draw a line to the word that goes with the clue.

1. This huge person shows up in fairy tales.   a. garden
2. You cannot hold this pet.   b. gap
3. This animal has a view from above.   c. giant
4. This is a game that is played on a green.   d. page
5. This is often planted in rows.   e. goldfish
6. A necklace could be made of this metal.   f. golf
7. This gets turned in a book.   g. giraffe
8. This is a space between things.   h. gold

C. Write a clue for the word *gerbil*.

_____

_____

Consonant Variants and Digraphs
Phonics

Name _____

Review It!

consonant variants
sounds of *g*

Fill in the circle by the word that best completes each sentence.

Gentle Giants

1. I like the tall _____ best of all the animals.
   - Ⓐ giraffe
   - Ⓑ goat
   - Ⓒ goose

2. Giraffes are the _____ of the animal world.
   - Ⓐ gates
   - Ⓑ gust
   - Ⓒ giants

3. Giraffes are _____. Most of them stand 18 feet tall!
   - Ⓐ game
   - Ⓑ stage
   - Ⓒ huge

4. Their coats can be a kind of orange and _____ color.
   - Ⓐ old
   - Ⓑ gold
   - Ⓒ large

5. Giraffes use their long necks to _____ food high up in trees.
   - Ⓐ gave
   - Ⓑ gap
   - Ⓒ gobble

6. A giraffe eats about 140 pounds of food every day. That's a _____ sum!
   - Ⓐ large
   - Ⓑ gone
   - Ⓒ range

7. Most of these giants live in _____ parks where they are safe.
   - Ⓐ gem
   - Ⓑ game
   - Ⓒ gone

8. Those giraffes are not kept in a _____.
   - Ⓐ cage
   - Ⓑ gate
   - Ⓒ gulf

Consonant Variants and Digraphs
Phonics

Learn It!
consonant variants

Name _____

Sounds of s

The consonant **s** often stands for the **/s/** sound.
The **s** can stand for the **/z/** sound, too.

Listen for the sound of **s** in the words below.

s has the /s/ sound	s has the /z/ sound
sing	dog**s**
le**ss**	ro**s**e

A. Read each word out loud. Draw a line to the sound of **s** that you hear.

silly   walls
parks   tops
please   **s has the /s/ sound**   sound
jumps   cheese
wise   **s has the /z/ sound**   soft
also   salt

B. Fill in the chart with your own words. The **/s/** sound of **s** is heard at the beginning, middle, or end of a word. The **/z/** sound of **s** is heard at the middle or end of a word.

s has the /s/ sound	s has the /z/ sound

Consonant Variants and Digraphs   83
Phonics

Practice It!

consonant variants
sounds of **s**

Name _____

Find Those Words!

A. Read the words out loud.
Underline the letter **s** in each word.
Write **s** where you hear the /s/ sound.
Write **z** where you hear the /z/ sound.

z ri<u>s</u>e	save	molds	salt	sing
walls	watches	soft	pants	runs

B. Circle the words above in the puzzle. The words can read down, across, or diagonally.

```
A  S  N  S  M  O  L  D  S  E  W
R  U  N  S  T  M  O  L  S  S  A
A  I  S  A  L  T  A  T  T  L  S
W  A  L  T  A  S  L  S  N  E  A
L  W  S  P  T  E  E  I  H  P  V
M  M  A  N  S  C  M  C  E  W  E
R  O  A  L  T  N  T  G  S  L  W
I  P  L  A  L  A  A  S  I  S  A
S  S  W  S  W  S  U  W  N  I  H
E  U  S  O  F  T  H  C  G  N  L
```

C. Write nine of the circled words on the lines.

_____ _____ _____

_____ _____ _____

_____ _____ _____

Review It!

consonant variants
sounds of **s**

Name _____

Fill in the circle by the word that best completes each sentence.

Sing Silly Songs

1. My scout troop had a _____ contest.
   - Ⓐ singing
   - Ⓑ sing
   - Ⓒ standing

2. My _____ Sara and I entered the contest.
   - Ⓐ mister
   - Ⓑ sister
   - Ⓒ Sam

3. Sara and I like to make up _____ songs.
   - Ⓐ seven
   - Ⓑ silly
   - Ⓒ soft

4. We change the _____ in songs that people know.
   - Ⓐ rings
   - Ⓑ walls
   - Ⓒ words

5. Sara and I sang about mold on _____.
   - Ⓐ cheese
   - Ⓑ chose
   - Ⓒ sun

6. People loved our _____.
   - Ⓐ mess
   - Ⓑ tries
   - Ⓒ ideas

7. I must say that we did _____ good, too.
   - Ⓐ send
   - Ⓑ sound
   - Ⓒ second

8. We were happy at the _____ that we were the winners.
   - Ⓐ songs
   - Ⓑ wise
   - Ⓒ news

Crazy for Candy Corn

Since she was little, Morgan loved Halloween. She loved the games. She loved dressing up. And she really loved the treats. There was one treat she loved most. Morgan was crazy about candy corn. She seemed to go through bags faster than a hungry dog with a bone.

Sometimes Morgan got sick from eating too many candy kernels. That's when she would decide never to eat candy corn again. But she always did!

Morgan's mom once took her to the place that made candy corn. They were surprised by the way the candy became the treat Morgan loved.

Morgan loved the taste. She saw that candy corn was made mostly of corn syrup and sugar. They gave the candy its sweet flavor.

Morgan also loved the corn shape and the three colors. She watched huge machines pour each color. The yellow, orange, and white flowed into molds one color at a time. The molds gave the candy its shape.

Morgan liked the way the candy was nice and shiny. She found out how it got that way. Large machines put a glaze of oil and wax on the candy. Then the candy was placed into large drums that tossed it around. The pieces rubbed gently against each other until they looked polished.

Of course, Morgan's very favorite thing about candy corn was eating it. So, at the end of the day, her mom bought a big bag at the gift shop. Morgan gobbled some pieces. Could it be? She was crazier than ever about candy corn!

Apply It!
consonant variants

Name _____

Now Try This...

1. Look back at the story. Write two words for each sound.

c has the /k/ sound		
g has the /j/ sound		
s has the /z/ sound		
c has the /s/ sound		
g has the /g/ sound		

2. Based on what you read, circle the sentence that is probably true.

   Morgan eats candy corn slowly so it lasts a long time.

   Morgan does not have much willpower.

   Morgan will no longer like candy corn when she grows up.

3. Would you let Morgan eat so much candy corn? Explain your answer.

   _____

   _____

4. Write the name of your favorite candy. _____
   Give two reasons why you like it.

   _____

   _____

5. Practice reading two paragraphs in the story. Then read them to your teacher.

Pretest
consonant digraphs
ch, sh, th, wh, ph, gh

Name _____

Read the first word in each row. Fill in the circle by the word that has the same sound as the underlined letters.

1. wa<u>sh</u>	Ⓐ batch	Ⓑ dashed	Ⓒ toss
2. <u>sh</u>ape	Ⓐ splash	Ⓑ chair	Ⓒ pitch
3. <u>ch</u>ip	Ⓐ school	Ⓑ ache	Ⓒ chase
4. tea<u>ch</u>	Ⓐ cot	Ⓑ chef	Ⓒ chin
5. <u>th</u>ank	Ⓐ Thomas	Ⓑ boathouse	Ⓒ bath
6. <u>th</u>at	Ⓐ gather	Ⓑ watch	Ⓒ with
7. <u>wh</u>ale	Ⓐ hoop	Ⓑ their	Ⓒ whisker
8. cou<u>gh</u>	Ⓐ through	Ⓑ laugh	Ⓒ ghost
9. <u>ph</u>one	Ⓐ gopher	Ⓑ perhaps	Ⓒ pony

Learn It!
consonant digraphs

Name _____

ch, sh, th, and wh

A digraph is two letters together that have one sound.

Listen for the consonant digraphs in these words:

cheese   da**sh**   ga**th**er   a**wh**ile

The letters **th** usually stand for the sound you hear in *south*.
The **th** also can stand for the sound you hear in *gather*.

A. Read each word out loud. Circle the consonant digraph.

bench	whale	whisper	shark
wheel	thin	fish	shape
child	gather	math	rich

B. In the first three rows, write the words that have the digraphs below. Use the words above. Then add your own words to the last two rows.

ch	sh	th	wh

Consonant Variants and Digraphs

Practice It!
consonant digraphs
ch, sh, th, wh

Name _____

Crossword Time!

A. Read each word out loud. Circle the letters that spell the consonant digraph.

finish	whale	chase	thunder	white
whisper	thirty	shapes	nothing	cash

B. Use words above to complete the crossword puzzle.

Down

1. a large mammal that lives in the sea
2. to speak very quietly
4. 3 x 10 = ___
5. the opposite of *something*
6. circles and triangles

Across

3. the color of fresh snow
4. a sound of a rainstorm
7. the end of a race
8. to run after

Review It!
consonant digraphs
ch, sh, th, wh

Name _____

Fill in the circle by the word that best completes each sentence.

How Many Shapes Do You Have?

1. Our class wanted to show the _____ grades that we love to read.
   - Ⓐ smother
   - Ⓑ other
   - Ⓒ rather

2. We got a large white _____ and hung it in the hallway.
   - Ⓐ sheet
   - Ⓑ sheep
   - Ⓒ shine

3. Then we made patches out of different pieces of _____.
   - Ⓐ chart
   - Ⓑ close
   - Ⓒ cloth

4. We cut the patches into _____.
   - Ⓐ shakes
   - Ⓑ shops
   - Ⓒ shapes

5. We glued a shape on the sheet for _____ book we had read.
   - Ⓐ each
   - Ⓑ teach
   - Ⓒ either

6. We used markers to write the book title and its _____ on the shape.
   - Ⓐ gather
   - Ⓑ bother
   - Ⓒ author

7. After a _____, the sheet had a lot of colorful pieces.
   - Ⓐ while
   - Ⓑ which
   - Ⓒ whisper

8. Martha reads all the time, so she had _____ shapes next to her name!
   - Ⓐ thirsty
   - Ⓑ thirty
   - Ⓒ third

Learn It!
consonant digraphs

Name _____

ph and gh

The digraph **ph** has the /f/ sound.
The digraph **gh** often has the /f/ sound.

Listen for the /f/ sound in these words:

gra**ph**   tou**gh**   **ph**one   ele**ph**ant

A. Read each word out loud. Circle the letters that spell the /f/ sound.

photo	telephone	rough	phase
laugh	cough	alphabet	tough
enough	graph	laughter	trophy

B. Use the words above to fill in the chart.

/f/ sound spelled *ph*	/f/ sound spelled *gh*

Consonant Variants and Digraphs
Phonics

Practice It!
consonant digraphs
ph, *gh*

Name _____

Tough Enough?

A. Read each word out loud. Circle the letters that spell the **/f/** sound.

> enough   elephant   photos   tough
>
> phone   rough   cough   alphabet

B. Read each clue. Then unscramble the answer and write it on the lines.

1. it might come with a cold — uoghc
2. used to make a call or take a photo — ponhe
3. an animal with a nose to its toes — pelehnta
4. a word for *pictures* — topsho
5. how an elephant's hide feels — rhugo
6. learned with a song — bpalhaet
7. "not easy" — gothu
8. "all you need" — egouhn

C. Unscramble the letters circled above to answer the clue.

You usually do not hear this sound during a test.

____ ____ ____ ____ ____ ____ ____

Review It!

consonant digraphs
ph, *gh*

Name _____

Fill in the circle by the word that best completes each sentence.

Fun with Photos

1. My dad loves to take _____ with his digital camera.

   Ⓐ photos   Ⓑ phones   Ⓒ phony

2. He has _____ photos to fill ten photo albums.

   Ⓐ enough   Ⓑ rough   Ⓒ cough

3. It is _____ for me to pick the best shots.

   Ⓐ graph   Ⓑ orphan   Ⓒ tough

4. I like the picture Dad took of his friend _____.

   Ⓐ Phone   Ⓑ Phil   Ⓒ Phase

5. Phil had a _____ day, so his hair was all messed up.

   Ⓐ enough   Ⓑ cough   Ⓒ rough

6. He put on a _____ red beard and made a silly face.

   Ⓐ phone   Ⓑ phony   Ⓒ phase

7. I also love the photo Dad calls "The _____ Joke," which he took when he and Mom went to Africa.

   Ⓐ Enough   Ⓑ Elephant   Ⓒ Laughter

8. The elephant is raising its trunk and looks as if it is _____!

   Ⓐ phoning   Ⓑ coughing   Ⓒ laughing

Read It!
consonant digraphs

A Whale to Watch

There are giants of the sea that make a 12,000-mile trip every year. Gray whales swim up and down the coast of North America. They feed in the north. They give birth in the south.

People who watch whales know how to spot a gray whale. Its skin is not pure gray. Hundreds of pounds of small shellfish attach themselves to the gray whale. They make the gray whale look as if it's covered in rough white patches. The gray whale has no top fin. Its fluke, or tail, has a notch down the middle.

A whale's breath escapes through a blowhole on the top of its head. The gray whale has a double blowhole shaped like the letter V. This whale's spout can rise about 15 feet in the air. The spout looks like a heart shape.

If you looked inside a gray whale's throat, you would not see any teeth. Like some other whales, the gray has two rows of baleen. The baleen looks like thick whiskers.

To eat, the whale opens its huge throat. It takes in tons of water and small shrimplike critters of the sea. The baleen forces out the water and mud. The food sticks to the baleen. The whale uses its giant tongue, as big as a car, to loosen the food and swallow it whole.

Grays dive for food in deep water, and they swim in shallow water, too. They usually give birth in shallow waters where there is little danger of sharks.

Grays, like other whales, can leap completely out of the water. Their massive bodies land with a gigantic splash. This action is called a breach because the whale breaks through the surface of the ocean. Some people think a gray whale breaches to get rid of some of its barnacles.

Apply It!
consonant digraphs

Name _____

Now Try This...

1. Look back at the story. Write four words for each digraph.

ch	sh	th	wh

2. What are two ways a gray whale's body is different from other whales?

_____

_____

3. What part of your face works like a whale's blowhole?

_____

_____

4. Find a word in the story that's new to you, or choose a word you like. Use the word in a sentence that shows you know what the word means.

_____

_____

5. Practice reading two paragraphs in the story. Then read them to your teacher.

Pretest
sounds of **ch**, **sh**, **ci**, **ti**

Name _____

Read the first word in each row. Fill in the circle next to the sound of the underlined letters.

1. <u>ch</u>op	Ⓐ /k/	Ⓑ /ch/	Ⓒ /sh/
2. bun<u>ch</u>	Ⓐ /k/	Ⓑ /ch/	Ⓒ /sh/
3. ma<u>ch</u>ine	Ⓐ /k/	Ⓑ /ch/	Ⓒ /sh/
4. s<u>ch</u>ool	Ⓐ /k/	Ⓑ /ch/	Ⓒ /sh/
5. <u>sh</u>ine	Ⓐ /ch/	Ⓑ /sh/	Ⓒ /z/
6. spla<u>sh</u>	Ⓐ /ch/	Ⓑ /sh/	Ⓒ /z/
7. <u>sh</u>ark	Ⓐ /sh/	Ⓑ /ch/	Ⓒ /z/
8. par<u>ti</u>al	Ⓐ /z/	Ⓑ /ch/	Ⓒ /sh/
9. ac<u>ti</u>on	Ⓐ /ch/	Ⓑ /sh/	Ⓒ /z/
10. deli<u>ci</u>ous	Ⓐ /sh/	Ⓑ /z/	Ⓒ /ch/

Consonant Variants and Digraphs
Phonics

Name _____

Learn It!
consonant digraphs

Sounds of ch

Most of the time, **ch** stands for the **/ch/** sound you hear in *chase*. Sometimes, **ch** has the **/sh/** sound or the **/k/** sound.

Listen for the sounds of **ch** in the words below.

/ch/	/sh/	/k/
chair	ma**ch**ine	stoma**ch**

A. Read each word out loud. Circle the **ch**. Then draw a line to the sound of **ch** you hear.

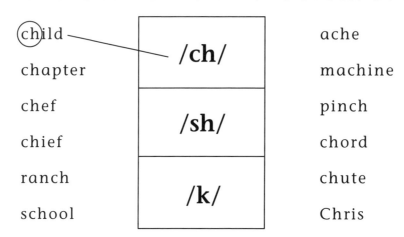

(ch)ild — /ch/
chapter
chef
chief — /sh/
ranch
school — /k/

ache
machine
pinch
chord
chute
Chris

B. Fill in the chart with words listed above.

ch has the /ch/ sound	ch has the /sh/ sound	ch has the /k/ sound

Consonant Variants and Digraphs
Phonics

Practice It!
consonant digraphs
sounds of **ch**

Name _____

What's the Word?

A. Read the words out loud.
Underline the **ch** in each word.
Write **ch** where you hear the **/ch/** sound.
Write **sh** where you hear the **/sh/** sound.
Write **k** where you hear the **/k/** sound.

ma<u>ch</u>ine (sh)	children	chase	stomach	lunch
sandwich	school	branch	chimps	chef

B. Write a word from above that goes with the definition.

1. another word for *belly*   _ _ _ _ _ _ _

2. the chief cook   _ _ _ _

3. a part of a tree that looks like its arm   _ _ _ _ _ _

4. a meal eaten in the middle of the day   _ _ _ _ _

5. slices of bread with food in between   _ _ _ _ _ _ _ _

6. small apes   _ _ _ _ _ _

7. to run after   _ _ _ _ _

8. young kids   _ _ _ _ _ _ _ _

C. Write a definition for the word *ache*.

_____

_____

Review It!

consonant digraphs
sounds of **ch**

Name _____

Fill in the circle by the word that best completes each sentence.

Check the Machine!

1. Have you ever lost _____ in a machine?
   - Ⓐ check
   - Ⓑ charms
   - Ⓒ change

2. I wanted a soda, so I found the soda _____ at the store.
   - Ⓐ chip
   - Ⓑ machine
   - Ⓒ chef

3. I put a _____ of quarters in the money slot.
   - Ⓐ hunch
   - Ⓑ cheek
   - Ⓒ bunch

4. Nothing came down, so I _____ the change button.
   - Ⓐ punched
   - Ⓑ lunched
   - Ⓒ choked

5. I _____ behind the flap, but there was no soda.
   - Ⓐ change
   - Ⓑ chopped
   - Ⓒ checked

6. It was time for _____, and I was hungry!
   - Ⓐ lunch
   - Ⓑ bunch
   - Ⓒ chef

7. I really wanted a drink to go with my peanut butter and jelly _____.
   - Ⓐ ranch
   - Ⓑ sandwich
   - Ⓒ machine

8. Finally, someone opened the machine and let me _____ a soda.
   - Ⓐ arch
   - Ⓑ stomach
   - Ⓒ choose

Consonant Variants and Digraphs
Phonics

Learn It!
variant spellings

The /sh/ Sound

The /sh/ sound can be spelled with **sh**, **ci**, or **ti**.

Listen for the /sh/ sound in these words:

shine   so**ci**al   na**ti**on

A. Read each word out loud. Circle the letters that spell the /sh/ sound.

special	addition	station	delicious
rushed	action	subtraction	share
motion	flashing	social	clash

B. Write words that show the spellings of the /sh/ sound. Use the words listed above.

/sh/ sound spelled *sh*	/sh/ sound spelled *ci*	/sh/ sound spelled *ti*

Practice It!
variant spellings
/sh/ sound

Name _____

Crossword Time!

A. Read each word out loud. Circle the two letters that spell the **/sh/** sound.

action	trash	fiction	special	shin
addition	rushed	delicious	motion	share

B. Use the words above to complete the crossword puzzle.

Down

1. front part of the leg
3. yummy
4. garbage
5. act of moving

Across

2. putting numbers together to get a sum
6. stories that are not real
7. not like others
8. hurried

Review It!

variant spellings
/sh/ sound

Name _____

Fill in the circle by the word that best completes each sentence.

One Solution

1. Shane's dad was _____ to see how much TV they watched every week.
   - Ⓐ rushed
   - Ⓑ shopped
   - Ⓒ shocked

2. "Shane, turn off that _____ so we can talk," said his dad.
   - Ⓐ social
   - Ⓑ action
   - Ⓒ station

3. "We need _____ ideas on how to spend our free time," Dad said.
   - Ⓐ fresh
   - Ⓑ flash
   - Ⓒ flesh

4. Shane and his dad agreed that they needed to take some _____.
   - Ⓐ share
   - Ⓑ action
   - Ⓒ suspicion

5. "This Friday, people across the _____ are not watching television," said Dad.
   - Ⓐ lotion
   - Ⓑ notion
   - Ⓒ nation

6. "I think we _____ join them," Dad went on.
   - Ⓐ ship
   - Ⓑ shine
   - Ⓒ should

7. "Well, I suppose that's one _____," said Shane.
   - Ⓐ solution
   - Ⓑ pollution
   - Ⓒ addition

8. On Friday, Shane and his dad took a _____ from TV.
   - Ⓐ addition
   - Ⓑ vacation
   - Ⓒ station

A Mission to Change

Chan did not like what he heard. It made his stomach ache. He was glad when the class session ended. Chan's teacher said that pollution hurt all living things. It even changed the climate. Pollution was found in every nation in the world!

Chan's voice was filled with emotion. "Pollution is out of control. We've got to take special action!" He and Chris were eating lunch.

"So what can we do?" asked Chris. He just wanted to eat his delicious sandwich.

"Well, we can start with Mr. Chapman. He wants someone to do his yardwork twice a month. We can do it. Let's use muscle power. No rides to his house. No machines that run on gas. No chemicals to feed his plants."

Chris hated the thought of so much work. But Chan had been his friend since the first day of school. Chris didn't want to let Chan down.

"You're on!" said Chris.

The boys got up early on Saturday. They rode their bikes to Mr. Chapman's house. Chan cut the grass with a push mower. Chris raked. They chopped fallen branches into smaller bits. Their arms ached. Their legs felt heavy like anchors. By the end of the day, they were moving in slow motion. Biking home was a chore.

The job went on for months. One Saturday, Chris showed off his upper arms. "Check these out!" he said.

Chan laughed. "We've made some good changes! We have cleaner air *and* stronger muscles!"

Apply It!
consonant digraphs

Name _____

Now Try This...

1. Look back at the story. Write three words that have the /k/ sound spelled **ch**.

   _____   _____   _____

2. Complete the chart with words from the story that have the /**sh**/ sound.

/sh/ spelled *ti*		
/sh/ spelled *ci*		

3. What kind of person is Chan? _____

   How can you tell? Use facts from the story.

   _____

   _____

4. What two things did Chan and Chris improve?

   _____

5. Do you think Chan and Chris did have an effect on pollution? Explain your answer.

   _____

   _____

6. Practice reading the first two paragraphs in the story. Then read them to your teacher.

Consonant Blends

Overview
The purpose of this section is to help students read words spelled with the three major groups of consonant blends: *r*-blends, *l*-blends, and *s*-blends. Because each of the consonants in a consonant blend is pronounced, most students will not have difficulty sounding out these words. Some students, however, may have trouble hearing the individual consonants.

Teaching Tips
You may want to use the following techniques for introducing the concepts in this section, starting with initial consonant blends:

Initial Blends pages 108–119
- Focus on one group of initial blends at a time, beginning with *r*-blends. Write the following words on the board:

    brim, crop, drape, grab, pry, trip

    Read each word out loud, blending the initial consonants as you run a finger under each letter. Have students do the same. Repeat the process with *l*-blends (e.g., *black, clock, flip, glue, plug*) and *s*-blends (e.g., *skip, slip, small, snap, spell, stop, swap*).

- Challenge students to make new words having blends by replacing the initial consonant of each word on the board with another letter (e.g., *brim* → *grim, prim, trim*).

Ending Blends pages 120–124
Repeat the process above using words such as:

bank, mold, camp, hint, rust, gift

Have students underline the ending blend in each word. Call attention to the letter/sound relationship of the consonants at the end of each word.

Rule Breakers
Consonant blends are highly reliable; they almost always stand for the blended sounds of each consonant. However, you may want to call students' attention to an exception: The letters *sc* can be a blend with the /**sk**/ sound, as in *score*, but they may also stand for the /**s**/ sound, as in *scent*. To avoid confusion, the letters *sc* are not introduced as a blend in this section.

Pretest
initial consonant blends
r-blends, *l*-blends

Name _____

Say the name of each picture. Write the letters that spell the blend you hear.

1.  ___ ___ ab

2.  ___ ___ anket

3. ___ ___ ug

4. ___ ___ ame

5.  ___ ___ obe

6. ___ ___ aces

7.  ___ ___ ash

8. ___ ___ ock

9.  ___ ___ apes

10.  ___ ___ ice

11. ___ ___ ag

12. ___ ___ ick

Learn It!
initial consonant blends

Name _____

Blends Spelled with a Consonant and an *r*

A consonant blend is two consonants together that are both said. For example, you say the *g* and the *r* sounds in *grill*.
An *r*-blend is made up of a consonant followed by an *r*.

Listen for the two sounds that begin these words:

brake   **cr**ib   **fr**ee   **pr**ice

A. Read each word out loud. Circle the two letters that spell the *r*-blend.

broke	cry	trick	pride	fresh
grade	brand	grab	crash	drag
trade	drive	press	Friday	treat

B. Write two words that begin with each *r*-blend. Use the words above. Then add your own words to the last two rows.

br____	dr____	gr____	pr____	tr____

Practice It!
initial consonant blends
r-blends

Name _____

Make It Match!

A. Read each word out loud. Circle the two letters that make the *r*-blend.

> brush   crate   drive   press   crab
>
> pride   tracks   frame   grades   Friday

B. Read each clue. Then draw a line to the word that goes with the clue.

1. This is the last day of the school week.   a. crab
2. You do this to a doorbell.   b. grades
3. Oranges are kept in this box.   c. Friday
4. This is a way to get from one place to another.   d. crate
5. These are on your report card.   e. brush
6. You can do this to your dog's fur.   f. tracks
7. A picture looks good in this.   g. press
8. This animal often walks sideways.   h. frame
9. These are the marks you leave in the snow.   i. drive
10. What you might feel when you have good grades.   j. pride

C. Write a clue for the word *treat*.

_____

_____

Review It!

initial consonant blends
r-blends

Name _____

Fill in the circle by the word that best completes each sentence.

Freddie's Braces

1. Freddie chewed some grape gum and _____ his braces.

    Ⓐ brave   Ⓑ broke   Ⓒ drove

2. "Grandpa!" Freddie _____ with panic.

    Ⓐ cried   Ⓑ crashed   Ⓒ crushed

3. "What's wrong, Freddie?" _____ asked as he came into the room.

    Ⓐ Great   Ⓑ Grandpa   Ⓒ Frame

4. "I broke my _____," Freddie said grimly.

    Ⓐ brisk   Ⓑ trades   Ⓒ braces

5. "We'll have to see our _____ Dr. Franklin so she can fix them," Grandpa said.

    Ⓐ friend   Ⓑ free   Ⓒ broken

6. "Do we have to?" Freddie asked with a _____.

    Ⓐ grape   Ⓑ grade   Ⓒ groan

7. "Tell the _____," Grandpa said. "Do you like Dr. Franklin?"

    Ⓐ trust   Ⓑ truth   Ⓒ track

8. "Dr. Franklin is _____," Freddie said, "but she'll be mad about the gum!"

    Ⓐ great   Ⓑ green   Ⓒ friend

Learn It!
initial consonant blends

Name _____

Blends Spelled with a Consonant and an *l*

An *l*-blend is made up of a consonant followed by an *l*.
In an *l*-blend, you say the sound of both consonants.
For example, you say the **b** and the **l** in **block**.

Listen for the two sounds that begin these words:

black **cl**ock **fl**ag **gl**ass **pl**ace

A. Read each word out loud. Circle the two letters that make the *l*-blend.

class	block	flip	plate	blimp
planet	globe	plum	flash	flame
bleed	clap	clam	glide	glance

B. Write three words that begin with each *l*-blend. Use the words above. Then add your own words to the last two rows.

bl___	cl___	fl___	gl___	pl___

Consonant Blends
Phonics

Practice It!
initial consonant blends
l-blends

Name _____

Fill in the Blanks

A. Read each word out loud. Circle the two letters that make the *l*-blend.

| planet | Club | class | Please | plan |
| glance | play | glad | block | blanket |

B. Read the poster. Fill in the missing words. Use words above.

Play for the Planet

Are you ready to play chess for a good cause? Our school cares about keeping the _____ Earth green. On Saturday, March 10, we're having Play for the Planet Day. Students from the Chess _____ will _____ chess all day long.

_____ join in the fun and sit down for a game! Or, you can promise money to back the players. Every cent will go to the recycling fund that our _____ has started. We have a _____ to start a recycling drive in May.

Tell everyone on your _____ to come and play and pledge. We know you will be _____ you helped keep our planet green!

Review It!

initial consonant blends
l-blends

Name _____

Fill in the circle by the word that best completes each sentence.

Please Bring a Blanket

1. On Saturday, our fifth-grade _____ is having a picnic.
   - Ⓐ clash
   - Ⓑ class
   - Ⓒ glass

2. We're going to the perfect _____ called Plume Park.
   - Ⓐ plan
   - Ⓑ flag
   - Ⓒ place

3. Each student will bring food and a _____ to sit on.
   - Ⓐ block
   - Ⓑ club
   - Ⓒ blanket

4. The school will have plenty of plastic _____ and cups for everyone.
   - Ⓐ planes
   - Ⓑ plates
   - Ⓒ blankets

5. It is not good to have anything made of _____ because it can break.
   - Ⓐ glass
   - Ⓑ grass
   - Ⓒ class

6. Our soccer _____ will bring what we need for a soccer game.
   - Ⓐ clue
   - Ⓑ frame
   - Ⓒ club

7. Mrs. Clancy will hang the school _____ near where we will meet.
   - Ⓐ block
   - Ⓑ flag
   - Ⓒ floss

8. The day _____ to be a lot of fun!
   - Ⓐ promises
   - Ⓑ props
   - Ⓒ pleads

Read It!
initial consonant blends

Honoring Grandmother

Crista groaned. She pleaded. She even cried. But her mother did not give in. No, Crista could not sleep over at Tracy's house. These were the Days of the Dead. They were a time to honor her grandmother.

Crista told Tracy that she had to go to a family party. She didn't say that the party would be in a cemetery.

The next day, Crista's family went to her grandmother's grave. They got right to work. Ray brushed away brittle leaves. Papa raked the ground. Crista and her mother pressed bright flowers into the soil. Soon the grave looked like a fluffy orange carpet. Papa set candles in clumps. Franco put Grandmother's picture near them.

Once the grave was ready, Mother asked Crista to spread the blankets. "It's time to eat," Mother said. The family shared Grandmother's favorite foods. The air smelled of spicy meats, fried beans, and sweet treats. Crista wished she were having pizza with Tracy.

Papa passed around special egg bread. Crista grabbed the loaf. She suddenly pictured her grandmother's kitchen. Grandmother liked Crista to help her make fresh bread. It was her job to shape the loaves.

Night came quickly. Crista glanced around the cemetery. It was crowded with families. It sounded as happy as a playground. Some people sang. Others played music. All the graves were lit with candles. Their light danced in the brisk night air.

Franco talked about Grandmother. She once had taken him on a long train ride to Mexico. The stories went on and on. They made Crista feel as if Grandmother were right there.

Crista felt proud. "I can't wait to tell Tracy about this party," she thought.

Apply It!
initial consonant blends

Name _____

Now Try This...

1. Look back at the story. Write two words that begin with each blend.

br___		
cr___		
fl___		
gr___		
pl___		

2. Name three ways the gathering at the cemetery was like a party.

_____
_____
_____

3. Why do you think Crista did not tell Tracy that her family was having a party in a cemetery?

_____
_____
_____

4. Why do you think Crista felt proud at the end of the story?

_____
_____

5. Practice reading two paragraphs in the story. Then read them to your teacher.

Pretest

initial consonant **s**-blends;
ending consonant blends

Name _____

Say the name of each picture. Write in the letters that spell the blend you hear.

1.  ___ ___ ake

2. ___ ___ ate

3.  ___ ___ oon

4.  ___ ___ amp

5. ___ ___ an

6.  ha ___ ___

7.  sku ___ ___

8.  pla ___ ___

9.  gi ___ ___

10.  te ___ ___

Consonant Blends
Phonics
116

Learn It!
initial consonant blends

Name _____

Blends Spelled with an *s* and a Consonant

An **s**-blend is made up of an **s** followed by a consonant. In an **s**-blend, you say the sound of both consonants. For example, you say the **s** and the **t** in **stick**.

Listen for the **s**-blends in these words:

skin **sn**ow **sp**end **sw**ish

A. Read each word out loud. Circle the two letters that spell the **s**-blend.

stop	sleeve	sting	slide	skill
spell	skate	swing	smoke	snack
stack	swim	skim	speed	smart

B. Write two words that begin with each **s**-blend. Use the words above. Then add your own words to the last row.

sl____	sm____	sp____	st____	sw____

Consonant Blends
Phonics

Practice It!
initial consonant blends
s-blends

Name _____

Find Those Words!

A. Read each word out loud. Circle the two letters that spell the **s**-blend.

| swing | stick | skating | snip |
| sleeve | step | smoke | spelling |

B. Circle the words above in the puzzle. The words can read down, across, or diagonally.

```
P  N  S  L  E  E  V  E  S  T
M  S  P  E  L  L  I  N  G  S
S  E  O  P  S  T  I  C  K  P
S  M  S  I  S  L  S  K  A  I
S  K  O  I  S  M  E  S  I  M
W  W  A  A  S  L  O  E  O  L
I  I  T  T  S  T  E  K  L  I
N  N  S  S  I  L  E  E  E  N
G  G  E  P  M  N  A  P  V  G
S  N  I  P  C  H  G  P  O  I
```

C. Write the circled words on the lines.

_____ _____ _____

_____ _____ _____

_____ _____

118 Consonant Blends
Phonics

Phonics and Word Study • EMC 3361 • © Evan-Moor Corp.

Review It!

initial consonant blends
s-blends

Name _____

Fill in the circle by the word that best completes each sentence.

Star Watch

1. Stan likes looking at the _____ in the night sky.
   - Ⓐ skunks
   - Ⓑ stops
   - Ⓒ stars

2. He loves to _____ time gazing through a telescope.
   - Ⓐ stand
   - Ⓑ spend
   - Ⓒ spent

3. Stan can _____ patterns of stars, such as the Big Dipper and Leo.
   - Ⓐ spy
   - Ⓑ sky
   - Ⓒ span

4. He knows that a lot of stars are in huge groups in _____.
   - Ⓐ spark
   - Ⓑ space
   - Ⓒ stick

5. He read that stars go through _____: they are born, they live, and they die.
   - Ⓐ sliders
   - Ⓑ stamps
   - Ⓒ stages

6. Stan says that most stars are _____ and cooler than the sun.
   - Ⓐ smaller
   - Ⓑ smellier
   - Ⓒ smarter

7. He likes to point out that all the stars _____ in space.
   - Ⓐ spot
   - Ⓑ spin
   - Ⓒ swim

8. Stan is really _____ when it comes to stars.
   - Ⓐ skate
   - Ⓑ smash
   - Ⓒ smart

Learn It!
ending consonant blends

Name _____

Consonant Blends at the Ends of Words

Many words end with consonant blends.
When you read a word with a consonant blend, you say the sound of each consonant.
For example, you say the **n** and the **t** in **bent**.

Listen to the blend at the end of each of these words:

so**ld** la**mp** me**lt** co**st**

A. Read each word out loud. Circle the two letters that spell the ending blend.

blank	plant	rest	left	bend
blend	swift	past	hint	mild
trunk	clump	brand	gold	camp

B. Write words that end with the blends. Use the words above.
Then add your own words to the last row.

____ft	____ld	____nk	____nt	____st

Practice It!
ending consonant blends

Name _____

What's the Word?

A. Read each word out loud. Circle the ending blend.

mist	drink	blend	ring	skunk
blimp	west	gold	invent	drift

B. Write **nd**, **ld**, **nt**, or **st** to form the word that goes with the clue. Read the word out loud.

1. You need more than one to clap.   h a ___ ___

2. If you enter this you might win a prize.   c o n t e ___ ___

3. This is something you don't want to catch.   c o ___ ___

4. Two of these make a quart.   p i ___ ___

5. This kind of person doesn't need a hairbrush.   b a ___ ___

6. A sandwich can have this part of the bread cut off.   c r u ___ ___

7. This is how you are marked when you are not at school.   a b s e ___ ___

8. This is the part of you that thinks.   m i ___ ___

C. Write a clue for the word *swamp*.

_____

_____

Review It!
ending consonant blinds

Name _____

Fill in the circle by the word that best completes each sentence.

The King's Ring

1. There once lived a king who had a gold _____.
   - Ⓐ rink
   - Ⓑ rang
   - Ⓒ ring

2. "I _____ it is time to clean my ring," the king said.
   - Ⓐ think
   - Ⓑ thing
   - Ⓒ blink

3. The king _____ his ring to the royal ring cleaner.
   - Ⓐ bent
   - Ⓑ sent
   - Ⓒ sold

4. When the king's _____ went to pick up the ring, it was gone!
   - Ⓐ invent
   - Ⓑ servant
   - Ⓒ gold

5. The royal ring cleaner was very upset. He knew the king was going to _____ him, or, perhaps, arrest him!
   - Ⓐ fold
   - Ⓑ behold
   - Ⓒ scold

6. "I know I left the ring in a small box right on this _____," the ring cleaner said.
   - Ⓐ shelf
   - Ⓑ first
   - Ⓒ swift

7. The ring cleaner saw something catch the light from his _____. He bent down to see what it was.
   - Ⓐ lent
   - Ⓑ stamp
   - Ⓒ lamp

8. "Here it is!" he cried. "Now I can _____ the servant home with the king's clean ring."
   - Ⓐ spend
   - Ⓑ send
   - Ⓒ stomp

Consonant Blends
Phonics

Read It!

initial consonant blends; ending consonant blends

Stella's Sled Ride

The smell of frying bacon woke Stella. This was her first winter camping trip with Gramps and Gran. Stella slipped on her warm clothes while she was still in her sleeping bag. Then she slid out from her cozy nest. She lifted the tent flap and stepped outside. The sky was clear blue.

After eating, Stella wanted to tie the dog Skipper to the dog sled. Stella wanted to go for a ride.

"Don't go far," said Gramps. "It might snow."

"Stick to the trails around the pond," said Gran. "The days were mild last week. Some of the ice may have started to melt."

"Okay," promised Stella. She jumped onto the back of the sled as Skipper started running. Stella held tightly as they sped around one bend and then another. When her feet got cold, Stella told Skipper to stop. She stamped her feet to warm them.

"We must be halfway around the pond by now," thought Stella. She saw a speck of orange across the pond. "That must be our tent."

Stella had not watched the sky. A wet snowflake landed on her nose. She looked up and saw a bank of gray clouds. "I think we better get back to camp," said Stella. "The quickest way is across the pond."

Stella ordered Skipper to move across the ice. The dog started forward. The ice squeaked. Skipper stopped. He backed up.

"Keep going!" yelled Stella. She got off the sled and tried to pull the dog. Skipper snapped and grabbed Stella's sleeve with his teeth. The strong dog pulled Stella back to shore just as the ice cracked. Skipper licked Stella's hand and wagged his tail.

"Wow!" said Stella. "Now take us home the best way. Stick to the path."

Consonant Blends
Phonics

Apply It!

initial consonant blends;
ending consonant blends

Name _____

Now Try This...

1. Look back at the story. Write words for each blend.

sl____	sp____	st____

____nd	____ld	____nk

2. Why did Stella want to cross the pond?

_____

_____

3. What might have happened if Stella had fallen through the pond's ice?

_____

_____

4. What is being compared to a "cozy nest" in the first paragraph? _____

   Why do you think it is called a cozy nest? _____

   _____

5. Practice reading a long paragraph in the story. Then read it to your teacher.

Vowel Digraphs and Other Letter Combinations

Overview
The purpose of this section is to help students read words containing a series of letters that stand for one sound. The section focuses primarily on digraphs, which are two-letter pairs that stand for one sound.

Teaching Tips
You may want to use the following techniques to introduce the concepts in this section:

Long Vowel Digraphs *pages 127–146*
Write a large **a** on a sticky-backed paper and a large **i** on another. Place the two letters apart from each other on the board. Have students sound out each letter as a long sound. Then move the letters side by side, and explain that they now make a new sound: **long a**, as in *pail* and *braid*. Ask students to suggest other words that have the **long a** sound spelled *ai*. Then repeat the process with other vowel pairs. Use letter combinations that stand for **long a**, *e*, *i*, *o*, or *u*, as introduced on pages 127–146. Give as many examples as you feel necessary for students to understand that the two letters make one sound. End with students suggesting other words with the same vowel digraphs.

Short Vowel Digraphs, Variants, and Other Letter Combinations *pages 148–164*
- This section includes the short vowel sounds of the vowel digraphs *ea*, *ui*, and *ou*. Write the following words on the board for students to copy:

    bread, build, cousin, touch, ahead

    Read each word out loud, and then underline the letter pair that stands for a short vowel sound. Then ask students to write *e*, *o*, or *u* above each vowel pair to indicate the vowel sound they hear.

- To introduce the variant digraph **oo,** write the following words on the board:

    moon, foot, cooks, loop, broom, shook

    Have students sort the words according to the two different sounds of **oo** they hear (**oo**, as in *wood*; **oo**, as in *cool*).

- To introduce the sounds of **ough,** write the following words on the board:

    though, cough, dough, ought, thought, although

    Have students sort the words according to the two different sounds of **ough** they hear (**long o**, as in *though*; **short o**, as in *cough*).

Rule Breakers
Short vowel digraphs can be difficult to decode because some letter pairs can stand for more than one sound. For example, *ea* has the **short e** sound in *head*, the **long e** sound in *bead*, and the **long a** sound in *great*. Keep students alert to exceptions in the English language, and explain that sometimes words must be read in context in order to determine their pronunciation.

Pretest

long vowel digraphs
ai, *ay*, *ea*, *ey*; *ea*, *ee*, *ey*, *ie*

Name _____

A. Read the words in each row. Fill in the circle next to the word with the **long a** sound.

1. Ⓐ crash Ⓑ track Ⓒ ramp Ⓓ grape

2. Ⓐ tap Ⓑ braid Ⓒ giant Ⓓ neat

3. Ⓐ anyway Ⓑ plant Ⓒ happy Ⓓ ready

4. Ⓐ sea Ⓑ plant Ⓒ dye Ⓓ break

5. Ⓐ west Ⓑ money Ⓒ obey Ⓓ talent

B. Read the words in each row. Fill in the circle next to the word with the **long e** sound.

1. Ⓐ since Ⓑ she Ⓒ her Ⓓ check

2. Ⓐ enter Ⓑ branches Ⓒ prince Ⓓ sweet

3. Ⓐ reader Ⓑ writer Ⓒ ahead Ⓓ hundred

4. Ⓐ children Ⓑ field Ⓒ science Ⓓ next

5. Ⓐ yellow Ⓑ desktop Ⓒ center Ⓓ monkey

Learn It!
long vowel digraphs

Name _____

> ### ai, ay, ea, ey
> A vowel digraph is made up of two vowels together that have one sound. The **long a** sound can be spelled: *ai*, *ay*, *ea*, *ey*.
>
> Listen for the **long a** sound in these words:
>
> br**ai**d   aw**ay**   br**ea**k   th**ey**

A. Read each word out loud. Circle the two letters that stand for the **long a** sound.

steak   trailer   remain   prey

freeway   tray   hey   outbreak

obey   always   paid   great

B. Use the words above to fill in the chart.

Long *a* spelled *ai*	Long *a* spelled *ay*	Long *a* spelled *ea*	Long *a* spelled *ey*

Practice It!
long vowel digraphs
ai, *ay*, *ea*, *ey*

Name _____

What's This?

A. Read each word out loud. Circle the two letters that stand for the **long a** sound.

> sailboat   subway   prey   mayor   brain
> daybreak   obey   Milky Way   afraid   steak

B. Write a word from above that goes with each clue.

1. This is a way to travel under the ground. _____
2. This is a way to travel on a lake. _____
3. This body part allows you to think and feel. _____
4. This is a cut of beef. _____
5. This animal is hunted by other animals. _____
6. This is the start of day. _____
7. This is made up of billions of stars. _____
8. This is the way to follow an order. _____
9. This is a way to react to bats. _____
10. This is the leader of a town or a city. _____

C. Write a "This is" clue for the word *chain*.

This is _____

Review It!

long vowel digraphs
ai, *ay*, *ea*, *ey*

Name _____

Fill in the circle by the word that best completes each sentence.

Stray Cat

1. Paige and her mom found a _____ cat in their yard one day.
    - Ⓐ spray
    - Ⓑ stay
    - Ⓒ stray

2. It had just _____, so the cat's fur was wet and slick.
    - Ⓐ rained
    - Ⓑ raided
    - Ⓒ raised

3. "I like its _____ gray markings," said Paige.
    - Ⓐ brain
    - Ⓑ plain
    - Ⓒ grain

4. "He looks as thin as a _____," Mom remarked.
    - Ⓐ pail
    - Ⓑ sail
    - Ⓒ rail

5. "We could give him some leftover _____," said Paige.
    - Ⓐ strain
    - Ⓑ stain
    - Ⓒ steak

6. "Don't be _____," Mom said as she petted the cat.
    - Ⓐ afraid
    - Ⓑ braid
    - Ⓒ maid

7. "If no one _____ him, can we keep him?" asked Paige.
    - Ⓐ paints
    - Ⓑ chains
    - Ⓒ claims

8. "Sure," said Mom. "Let's put an ad in the paper without _____."
    - Ⓐ decay
    - Ⓑ delay
    - Ⓒ display

Learn It!
long vowel digraphs

Name _____

ea, ee, ey, ie

The **long e** sound can be spelled: **ea**, **ee**, **ey**, **ie**.

Listen for the **long e** sound in these words:

t**ea**ch   agr**ee**   k**ey**   sh**ie**ld

A. Read each word out loud. Circle the two letters that stand for the **long e** sound.

teeth	donkey	feet	yield
money	chief	dream	honey
beak	needle	meal	believe

B. Use the words above to fill in the first three rows. Then add your own words to the last row.

Long *e* spelled *ea*	Long *e* spelled *ee*	Long *e* spelled *ey*	Long *e* spelled *ie*

Practice It!
long vowel digraphs
ea, *ee*, *ey*, *ie*

Name _____

Find Those Words!

A. Read each word out loud. Circle the two letters that stand for the **long e** sound.

| needle | meat | donkey | shield | wheat |
| cookie | money | creep | sweet | beads |

B. Circle the words above in the puzzle. The words can read down, across, or diagonally.

```
H  C  C  R  N  E  E  D  L  E  H
C  O  O  K  I  S  D  T  W  A  E
N  H  T  O  D  T  E  A  W  H  B
H  E  E  A  K  T  Y  S  H  B  E
C  R  E  E  P  I  S  H  E  M  A
D  B  T  L  T  E  E  I  A  A  D
O  I  T  A  I  D  M  E  T  A  S
N  E  E  U  L  O  R  L  R  C  C
K  M  B  I  N  T  R  D  L  W  R
E  O  H  E  H  A  D  A  N  K  E
Y  S  Y  W  E  S  W  E  E  T  T
```

C. Write nine of the circled words on the lines.

_____ _____ _____

_____ _____ _____

_____ _____ _____

Review It!

long vowel digraphs
ea, *ee*, *ey*, *ie*

Name _____

Fill in the circle by the word that best completes each sentence.

A Sweet Pet

1. My friend Stevie has a pet _____ named Sweetie.
   - Ⓐ monkey
   - Ⓑ money
   - Ⓒ key

2. Stevie taught Sweetie how to do tricks for _____.
   - Ⓐ team
   - Ⓑ feet
   - Ⓒ treats

3. If Stevie _____ through his alarm, Sweetie wakes him up.
   - Ⓐ steeps
   - Ⓑ weeps
   - Ⓒ sleeps

4. At first, Stevie thinks he's _____, but then the monkey squeaks and squeals.
   - Ⓐ creeping
   - Ⓑ dreaming
   - Ⓒ hearing

5. Stevie always says, "Good monkey," and then gives Sweetie a _____ as a treat.
   - Ⓐ cookie
   - Ⓑ shield
   - Ⓒ money

6. These cookies are good for monkeys and help keep their _____ clean.
   - Ⓐ feet
   - Ⓑ sweet
   - Ⓒ teeth

7. Someone once offered to buy Sweetie for a lot of _____.
   - Ⓐ sleep
   - Ⓑ honey
   - Ⓒ money

8. Stevie said no, because he wants to _____ Sweetie forever.
   - Ⓐ treat
   - Ⓑ keep
   - Ⓒ creep

Read It!
long vowel digraphs

CREATURES of the DEEP

The sea is home to a lot of odd creatures. Some look silly with mouths shaped like beaks. Others look fierce with long teeth as sharp as needles.

The sea horse is a strange sea creature. Its name comes from the shape of its head. Sea horses are weak swimmers. They live among sea plants like seaweed. Sea horses stay in one place by curling their tails around the plants.

Moray eels like to remain in one place, too. These fish look like snakes. They can hide their long bodies among reefs and rocks. The rocks shield the eels from danger. The moray eel waits for its dinner to swim by. Then it opens its wide mouth. It uses its sharp teeth to grab its prey.

The moray always opens and closes its mouth to breathe. Showing those sharp teeth makes the fish look mean.

The ray is another strange fish. It looks like a flat disk with wings. Most rays have very long tails. Stingrays have spines on their tails. The spines can cause painful cuts.

The sea star is another sea animal with spines. Most sea stars have five arms. If an arm breaks off, another grows back. Sea stars also have rows of tube feet. They use these feet to creep around the sea.

Sea snails do not swim or creep. They glide on one flat foot! They move around slowly and feed off dead plants and animals.

People eat sea snails and other sea creatures, like crab. People pay a lot of money for these sweet meats. It seems that sea life can be strange *and* tasty!

Apply It!
long vowel digraphs

Name _____

Now Try This...

1. Look back at the story. Write four words for each digraph.

ai	ay	ea (long *e* sound)	ee

2. Read each set of clues out loud. Write the name of the sea creature the clues describe.

   a. long body, reef, remains in place _____

   b. weak, seaweed, curls tail _____

   c. tube feet, arms, creeps _____

   d. eaten, sweet meat, glides _____

3. What might happen if you bothered a moray eel?

   _____

   _____

4. What sea creature do you think is strange? _____

   Why? _____

   _____

5. Practice reading two paragraphs in the story. Then read them to your teacher.

Pretest

long vowel digraphs: *ie*, *uy*, *ye*;
oa, *oe*, *ow*; *ew*, *ue*
letter combinations: *igh*

Name _____

A. Read the words in each row. Fill in the circle next to the word with the **long i** sound.

1. Ⓐ tip   Ⓑ tied   Ⓒ tune   Ⓓ lip
2. Ⓐ ships   Ⓑ slips   Ⓒ night   Ⓓ noise
3. Ⓐ buy   Ⓑ boy   Ⓒ pony   Ⓓ pill
4. Ⓐ money   Ⓑ dye   Ⓒ trip   Ⓓ digging

B. Read the words in each row. Fill in the circle next to the word with the **long o** sound.

1. Ⓐ some   Ⓑ light   Ⓒ sloppy   Ⓓ soap
2. Ⓐ tops   Ⓑ ties   Ⓒ toes   Ⓓ cartoon
3. Ⓐ crow   Ⓑ how   Ⓒ too   Ⓓ tune

C. Read the words in each row. Fill in the circle next to the word with the **long u** sound.

1. Ⓐ gust   Ⓑ glue   Ⓒ glum   Ⓓ gum
2. Ⓐ file   Ⓑ float   Ⓒ flew   Ⓓ funny
3. Ⓐ overdue   Ⓑ beads   Ⓒ bunny   Ⓓ sunny

Learn It!

long vowel digraphs;
letter combinations

Name _____

ie, igh, uy, ye

The **long i** sound can be spelled *ie*, *igh*, *uy*, or *ye*.

Listen for the **long i** sound in these words:

tr**ie**d   l**igh**t   g**uy**   b**ye**

A. Read each word out loud. Circle the letters that spell the **long i** sound.

dye	buy	guys	rye
night	lye	lie	high
sigh	bright	died	pie

B. Use the words above to fill in the chart.

Long *i* spelled *ie*	Long *i* spelled *igh*	Long *i* spelled *uy*	Long *i* spelled *ye*

Practice It!

long vowel digraphs: *ie*, *uy*, *ye*;
letter combinations: *igh*

Name _____

What's the Right Match?

A. Read each word out loud. Circle the letters that spell the **long i** sound.

pie	right	buys	dye	lie
light	guy	rye	sigh	highlight

B. Draw a line from each definition to a **long i** word for a match.

1. to change the color of something   a. rye
2. gets something by paying money for it   b. lie
3. grain used to make flour   c. guy
4. to breathe out deeply   d. buys
5. to get into a flat position   e. dye
6. a man or a boy   f. right
7. to mark with bright-colored ink   g. sigh
8. side opposite the left   h. highlight
9. a dessert with a filling   i. light
10. not dark; bright   j. pie

C. Write a definition for the word *pie*.

_____

_____

Vowel Digraphs and Other Letter Combinations

Review It!

long vowel digraphs: **ie**, **uy**, **ye**;
letter combinations: **igh**

Name _____

Fill in the circle by the word that best completes each sentence.

Night Flight

1. Brighton hugged her dog and said, "_____, Popeye."

   Ⓐ Buy   Ⓑ Bright   Ⓒ Bye

2. Hating to leave her pet, Brighton let out a deep _____.

   Ⓐ high   Ⓑ sigh   Ⓒ nigh

3. She was heading to Ireland on a late _____ from New York City.

   Ⓐ fright   Ⓑ flight   Ⓒ fight

4. It would be _____ when the plane landed in Cork, Ireland.

   Ⓐ highlight   Ⓑ headlight   Ⓒ daylight

5. Brighton got on the plane, found her seat, and _____ to relax.

   Ⓐ tried   Ⓑ cried   Ⓒ dried

6. She thought she knew the _____ sitting in the row across from her.

   Ⓐ buy   Ⓑ guy   Ⓒ lie

7. Brighton undid her seatbelt once the plane was flying _____ enough.

   Ⓐ sigh   Ⓑ high   Ⓒ thigh

8. As the plane began to land, she enjoyed the _____ of the green fields.

   Ⓐ right   Ⓑ bright   Ⓒ sight

Learn It!
long vowel digraphs

Name _____

oa, oe, ow

The **long o** sound can be spelled **oa**, **oe**, or **ow**.

Listen for the **long o** sound in these words:

m**oa**n   w**oe**s   wind**ow**

A. Read each word out loud. Circle the two letters that stand for the **long o** sound.

thrown	soap	doe	float
toe	follow	slowly	boast
crow	foe	oak	Joe

B. Use the words above to fill in the first four rows. Then add your own words to the last row.

Long *o* spelled *oa*	Long *o* spelled *oe*	Long *o* spelled *ow*

Practice It!
long vowel digraphs
oa, *oe*, *ow*

Name _____

Crossword Time!

A. Read the words out loud. Circle the two letters that stand for the **long o** sound.

window	stows	float	doe	toast
tows	soap	slowly	yellow	woes

B. Use the words above to complete the crossword puzzle.

Down

1. the color of a honeybee
3. puts away or stores in a place
4. problems
6. pulls something behind
7. to stay on top of water

Across

2. good with butter or jam
4. it can be opened for air
5. female deer
8. not quickly
9. it gets rid of grime

Review It!
long vowel digraphs
oa, *oe*, *ow*

Name _____

Fill in the circle by the word that best completes each sentence.

A Slow Yellow Boat

1. My family _____ a yellow boat that we keep on a lake.
   - Ⓐ owes
   - Ⓑ throws
   - Ⓒ owns

2. The boat is large, but it moves very _____.
   - Ⓐ tow
   - Ⓑ glowing
   - Ⓒ slowly

3. Mom _____ we like to sleep on the boat, so we spend some weekends at the lake.
   - Ⓐ shows
   - Ⓑ knows
   - Ⓒ slows

4. I sleep on the top bunk and my little brother sleeps _____ me.
   - Ⓐ below
   - Ⓑ bowl
   - Ⓒ tow

5. Sometimes my brother reaches up from his bed and tickles my _____.
   - Ⓐ toes
   - Ⓑ tows
   - Ⓒ floats

6. "Stop it," I _____. My brother can be such a pest!
   - Ⓐ soak
   - Ⓑ roam
   - Ⓒ moan

7. There's a window next to my bed, so I watch animals _____ the hills.
   - Ⓐ foam
   - Ⓑ roam
   - Ⓒ foal

8. I also like to watch the water birds _____ on the lake.
   - Ⓐ flow
   - Ⓑ float
   - Ⓒ snow

Learn It!
long vowel digraphs

Name _____

ew, ue

The **long u** sound often is spelled **ew**.
The **long u** also can be spelled **ue**.

Listen for the **long u** sound in these words:

fl**ew**   gl**ue**

A. Read each word out loud. Circle the two letters that stand for the **long u** sound.

grew	cue	true	threw
news	crew	few	clue
fuel	hue	argue	jewel

B. Use the words above to fill in the chart.

Long *u* spelled *ew*	Long *u* spelled *ue*

Vowel Digraphs and Other Letter Combinations
Phonics

Practice It!
long vowel digraphs
ew, *ue*

Name _____

Word Scramble

A. Read each word out loud. Circle the two letters that stand for the **long u** sound.

> value   glue   overdue   clues
>
> untrue   news   renew   chew

B. Read each clue about books. Then unscramble the answer and write it on the lines.

1. what make-believe stories are   unetur   __ __ __ __ __ __
2. mice might do this to book pages   ewhc   __ __ __ __
3. you look for these when reading a mystery   sluce   __ __ __ __ __
4. you do this to keep library books longer   wenre   __ __ __ __ __
5. used to attach pages to the spine of a book   legu   __ __ __ __
6. books returned late to the library   veroued   __ __ __ __ __ __ __
7. what some true books may have   swen   __ __ __ __

C. Use the word *interview* to tell about someone you would like to meet. Explain why.

_____

_____

_____

Review It!

long vowel digraphs
ew, *ue*

Name _____

Fill in the circle by the word that best completes each sentence.

We Grew a Stew

1. Have you ever eaten something that you _____ was special?
   - Ⓐ knew
   - Ⓑ grew
   - Ⓒ true

2. Our class _____ vegetables in a small garden.
   - Ⓐ brew
   - Ⓑ glue
   - Ⓒ grew

3. It is _____ that if you take care of plants, they will grow.
   - Ⓐ pew
   - Ⓑ clue
   - Ⓒ true

4. We worked hard and _____ out weeds that grew there.
   - Ⓐ news
   - Ⓑ threw
   - Ⓒ blue

5. The plants grew fast during the weeks of sunny days and _____ skies.
   - Ⓐ flew
   - Ⓑ blue
   - Ⓒ news

6. Then we looked for _____ that the vegetables were ripe.
   - Ⓐ glues
   - Ⓑ news
   - Ⓒ clues

7. We used the ripe veggies to make a tasty _____ for lunch.
   - Ⓐ stew
   - Ⓑ shrew
   - Ⓒ sue

8. No one could _____. It sure was a tasty stew!
   - Ⓐ chew
   - Ⓑ argue
   - Ⓒ view

Read It!

long vowel digraphs; letter combinations

A Trail of Clues

Joe woke up and raced downstairs. It was a beautiful day for a birthday! His family was eating oatmeal and toast, just like always. Where were the balloons? Where was the cake? How about the gifts? Did his family think Joe was too old for birthday fun?

The doorbell rang. "I'll get it!" Joe cried. He was sure his friends had come by. When Joe opened the door, no one was there. A newspaper lay on the ground. Joe picked it up. Then he saw a note taped to the door. It read:

We tiptoed here with some clues.
Find the first one in the news.

A treasure hunt! What a great idea! Joe flipped through the newspaper. He saw a note written on blue paper:

To find your next clue, birthday fellow,
set your sights on something yellow.

Joe moaned. He could see lots of yellow things. One by one he searched them all. Finally, he climbed up his little sister's slide. There was the clue:

Look in the coat of a thing that might
frighten the crows so they take flight!

Joe dashed next door. A scarecrow stood in the garden. Sure enough, another clue was in its coat pocket.

Joe spent the rest of the morning following one clue after another. He found one in an oak tree and one tied to a snowblower. He found the last clue buried in his sister's sandbox:

The game's over. It's sad but true.
We're here to say Happy Birthday to you!

The treasure hunt was over. But there was no treasure! Joe sighed and walked slowly into the house. He decided to spend the rest of the day in his room.

"Surprise! Happy Birthday!" Joe's family and friends yelled. Joe smiled. He would never outgrow birthday fun.

Vowel Digraphs and Other Letter Combinations

Apply It!

long vowel digraphs;
letter combinations

Name _____

Now Try This...

1. Look back at the story. Write three words for each set of letters.

igh	*oa*	*ow*	*ue*

2. Why do you think Joe's family and friends planned the treasure hunt?

_____

_____

3. How did Joe's feelings change during the story?

At first, Joe was _____ when _____

_____.

Then, Joe was _____ when _____

_____.

4. Why did Joe's feelings change?

_____

_____

5. Practice reading two paragraphs in the story. Then read them to your teacher.

Pretest

short vowel digraphs: **ea**, **ui**, **ou**;
variant digraphs: **au**, **aw**

Name _____

Read the first word in each row. Fill in the circle by the word that has the same vowel sound as the underlined letters.

1. r<u>ea</u>dy	Ⓐ meal	Ⓑ dread	Ⓒ teach
2. thr<u>ea</u>d	Ⓐ beak	Ⓑ dream	Ⓒ instead
3. b<u>ui</u>lt	Ⓐ ruin	Ⓑ building	Ⓒ child
4. g<u>ui</u>lt	Ⓐ build	Ⓑ suit	Ⓒ quite
5. r<u>ou</u>gh	Ⓐ round	Ⓑ shout	Ⓒ tough
6. t<u>ou</u>ch	Ⓐ though	Ⓑ country	Ⓒ through
7. bec<u>au</u>se	Ⓐ draw	Ⓑ player	Ⓒ candy
8. c<u>au</u>ght	Ⓐ taught	Ⓑ laugh	Ⓒ nature
9. cl<u>aw</u>	Ⓐ grown	Ⓑ cause	Ⓒ track
10. l<u>aw</u>n	Ⓐ layer	Ⓑ laugh	Ⓒ laws

Learn It!
short vowel digraphs

Name _____

ea, ui, ou

Some vowel digraphs stand for short vowel sounds.

The digraph **ea** sometimes stands for the **short e** sound as in *head*.
The digraph **ui** sometimes stands for the **short i** sound as in *built*.
The digraph **ou** sometimes stands for the **short u** sound as in *cousin*.

A. Read each word out loud. Circle the letters that spell a short vowel sound.

thread	buildings	rough	ready
young	meadow	country	guilt
instead	touch	spread	enough

B. Use the words above to fill in the chart.

Short *e* spelled *ea*	Short *i* spelled *ui*	Short *u* spelled *ou*

Vowel Digraphs and Other Letter Combinations
Phonics
148

Practice It!
short vowel digraphs
ea, *ui*, *ou*

Name _____

Fill in the Blanks

A. Read each word out loud. Circle the letters that spell the **short e**, **short i**, or **short u** sound.

enough	build	spread	ready
country	already	Instead	tough

B. Read the speech. Write in the missing words. Use the words above.

I want to tell you that I am against the building plan for our town. I think we have _____ buildings. Right now, someone is planning to _____ a large hotel near North Reading Park. We _____ have a lot of traffic on Main Street. It is _____ to park downtown. If we add a hotel, traffic will be a problem.

A large hotel would bring more people to our town. The hotel could also bring people to the towns around us. The traffic problem could _____ to the whole area.

I do not think we are _____ for such a big change. We live in one of the nicest towns in the whole _____. We should not rush to make choices. _____, let us take some time to study the building plan and see if it is good for our town.

Review It!

short vowel digraphs
ea, *ui*, *ou*

Name _____

Fill in the circle by the word that best completes each sentence.

Heading to the Country

1. Dad packed the car and asked if all of us were _____ to go.

   Ⓐ ready Ⓑ steady Ⓒ rough

2. We'd had _____ of the city, and we were ready to get out of town.

   Ⓐ tough Ⓑ enough Ⓒ touch

3. It was early Friday afternoon, and the traffic was _____ backed up.

   Ⓐ death Ⓑ breath Ⓒ already

4. "I _____ sitting in traffic," Dad said. "It's such a waste of our time."

   Ⓐ thread Ⓑ instead Ⓒ dread

5. "Let's try going on the back roads _____," Mom said.

   Ⓐ steady Ⓑ instead Ⓒ head

6. "Those roads are poor and can be really _____ on the car," Dad replied.

   Ⓐ cough Ⓑ head Ⓒ rough

7. "I read that new roads were _____ in the past year," Mom said.

   Ⓐ guilt Ⓑ built Ⓒ suit

8. "So the choice isn't so _____," said Dad. "We're taking the back roads!"

   Ⓐ tough Ⓑ builds Ⓒ enough

Learn It!
variant vowel digraphs

Name _____

au, aw

The digraphs **au** and **aw** both stand for the same vowel sound.

Listen for the **au** and **aw** sound in these words:

author   h**aw**k   h**au**l   sh**aw**l

A. Read each word out loud. Circle the two letters that stand for one vowel sound.

straw	because	launch	fault
claw	sawed	lawn	sauce
August	paws	pause	yawn

B. Use the words above to fill in the chart.

Vowel sound spelled *au*	Vowel sound spelled *aw*

Practice It!
variant vowel digraphs
au, *aw*

Name _____

One Way...

A. Read each word out loud. Circle the two letters that stand for one vowel sound.

paws	pause	launch	claws	awful
haul	crawl	yawn	drawer	Austin

B. Draw lines to match the clues to the words.

1. one way to move a large load — a. launch
2. one way to show you are tired — b. Austin
3. one way to move through a cave — c. pause
4. one way to make a DVD stop — d. claws
5. one way a bear goes up a tree — e. haul
6. one way you might feel when a friend moves away — f. yawn
7. one way to name a boy — g. awful
8. one way to send a rocket into space — h. crawl

C. Write a "one way" clue for the word *draw*.

one way _____

_____

_____

Review It!

variant vowel digraphs
au, *aw*

Name _____

Fill in the circle by the word that best completes each sentence.

Paws and Claws

1. I love anything with four _____ and a tail.
   - Ⓐ saws
   - Ⓑ paws
   - Ⓒ straws

2. I help out at Dr. Austin's office, _____ I want to be a vet one day.
   - Ⓐ because
   - Ⓑ cause
   - Ⓒ claws

3. This job will help _____ my work as an animal doctor.
   - Ⓐ haul
   - Ⓑ lawn
   - Ⓒ launch

4. Dr. Austin has shown me how to groom cats and clip their _____.
   - Ⓐ laws
   - Ⓑ claws
   - Ⓒ saws

5. Last week, Dr. Austin found a stray puppy on the office _____.
   - Ⓐ lawn
   - Ⓑ launch
   - Ⓒ awful

6. She had to _____ on the ground so she would not scare the puppy.
   - Ⓐ thaw
   - Ⓑ crawl
   - Ⓒ yawn

7. Dr. Austin brought the puppy inside, and we gave it a bath under the _____.
   - Ⓐ cloud
   - Ⓑ drawer
   - Ⓒ faucet

8. When I _____ the puppy, I knew why I liked working with a vet.
   - Ⓐ draw
   - Ⓑ hauled
   - Ⓒ saw

Vowel Digraphs and Other Letter Combinations
Phonics

Read It!
short vowel digraphs and variants

CAUGHT!

Heather loved the month of August. That's when she visited her Aunt Maude and cousin Dawn. They lived in a home near a meadow. Dawn recently got a young cat named Jigsaw.

When Heather arrived this summer, Dawn pulled her aside. She whispered, "I've been hearing scratching sounds. I thought Jigsaw was clawing at my door last night. So I opened it. Jigsaw wasn't there!"

Dawn took a deep breath. "Then today I was in the kitchen. Jigsaw jumped near the sink. He tapped his paw on the faucet. I thought he wanted a drink, so I turned on the tap. Then the scratching started! I looked under the sink. Nothing was there."

That night, Heather heard the scratching. She imagined a monster trying to claw its way into her room. It was an awful night.

Heather woke up to the smell of fresh bread. There were two hot loaves ready for breakfast.

As she began setting the table, Heather paused. She saw a small shape. It dashed out from under the sink. Then it crawled up the counter to the bread. "I know what's been making the scratching sounds!" said Heather.

Everyone looked at the bread. A guinea pig sat eating it.

"That's Austin's guinea pig!" said Dawn. She picked it up. "Austin came by a day ago to show it to me. When he got home, his guinea pig wasn't in its cage. Austin thought he had lost it in the meadow."

Heather laughed. "This could be the first time that bread helped catch a guilty party!"

Apply It!
short vowel digraphs and variants

Name _____

Now Try This...

1. Look back at the story. Write three words for each sound.

/ea/ (short *e* as in *head*)			
/au/			
/aw/			

2. Write a story word for each of these sounds:

/ui/ (short *i* as in *built*)	
/ou/ (short *u* as in *rough*)	

3. Why do you think Heather felt that a monster was clawing into her room?

_____

_____

4. Why do you think the guinea pig was scratching on the walls?

_____

_____

5. How did the bread "catch" the guinea pig?

_____

_____

6. Practice reading two paragraphs in the story. Then read them to your teacher.

Pretest

**variant vowel digraphs: oo;
letter combinations: ough**

Name _____

Read the first word in each row. Fill in the circle by the word that has the same sound as the underlined letters.

1. g<u>oo</u>d	Ⓐ tool	Ⓑ droop	Ⓒ foot
2. b<u>oo</u>t	Ⓐ tooth	Ⓑ shook	Ⓒ books
3. c<u>oo</u>kie	Ⓐ smooth	Ⓑ football	Ⓒ mood
4. sch<u>oo</u>l	Ⓐ notebook	Ⓑ cook	Ⓒ zoom
5. br<u>oo</u>m	Ⓐ noon	Ⓑ wood	Ⓒ good-bye
6. r<u>ough</u>	Ⓐ though	Ⓑ tough	Ⓒ would
7. d<u>ough</u>	Ⓐ ought	Ⓑ cough	Ⓒ though
8. b<u>ough</u>t	Ⓐ cloud	Ⓑ thought	Ⓒ rough

156 Vowel Digraphs and Other Letter Combinations
Phonics

Phonics and Word Study • EMC 3361 • © Evan-Moor Corp.

Learn It!
variant vowel digraphs

Name _____

Sounds of *oo*

The digraph **oo** can stand for the vowel sound you hear in *wood*.
The **oo** also can stand for the vowel sound you hear in *cool*.
Try both sounds when you come to a word you don't know.

Listen for the sounds of **oo** in the words below.

oo sound as in *wood*	*oo* sound as in *cool*
c**oo**k	r**oo**ts
st**oo**d	sch**oo**l

A. Read each word out loud. Circle the words that have the **oo** sound you hear in *wood*. Underline the words that have the **oo** sound you hear in *cool*.

zoom	notebook	moose	spoon
books	hooked	shook	boots
football	gloomy	coop	brook

B. Use the words above to fill in the first four rows of the chart. Then add your own words to the last row.

oo sound as in *wood*	*oo* sound as in *cool*

Vowel Digraphs and Other Letter Combinations
Phonics

Practice It!
variant vowel digraphs
sounds of **oo**

Name _____

Rhyme Time!

A. Read each word out loud. Circle the words that have the **oo** sound you hear in *wood*. Underline the words that have the **oo** sound you hear in *cool*.

school	room	cooked	scoop	book
looked	soon	snoop	took	noon

B. Read the poem. Write words from above to finish the rhymes.

I felt like a fool
Last Friday at _____.

I thought some crook
Had taken my _____.

I looked and I looked
Thinking, "My goose is _____!"

My brother, the snoop,
Said, "Hey, here's the _____.

You left so soon
When the bell rang at _____.

Your book's in the _____.
Just ask Ms. Bloom."

Review It!

variant vowel digraphs
sounds of **oo**

Name _____

Fill in the circle by the word that best completes each sentence.

Aunt Oona

1. I think my Aunt Oona is really _____.

   Ⓐ pool   Ⓑ cool   Ⓒ hoot

2. She's a well-known carpenter who works with _____.

   Ⓐ spool   Ⓑ foot   Ⓒ wood

3. Aunt Oona has a workshop full of _____.

   Ⓐ tools   Ⓑ spoons   Ⓒ brooms

4. I have spent lots of _____ watching Aunt Oona at work.

   Ⓐ childhoods Ⓑ noons   Ⓒ afternoons

5. She first checks that each piece of wood is not _____.

   Ⓐ proofed   Ⓑ crooked   Ⓒ hooked

6. She saws, cuts, trims, and sands the wood to a _____ finish.

   Ⓐ gloomy   Ⓑ smooth   Ⓒ stood

7. She collects _____ from the beach and makes it into tables, too.

   Ⓐ driftwood   Ⓑ childhood   Ⓒ grooms

8. Aunt Oona sells so much of her work that I think she will _____ be famous.

   Ⓐ soon   Ⓑ boom   Ⓒ bloom

Learn It!
letter combinations

Name _____

Sounds of *ough*

The letters **ough** all together can stand for different sounds.

Listen for two different sounds of **ough** in these words:

Long *o* sound	Short *o* sound
th**ough**	c**ough**

A. Read each word out loud. Circle the letters **ough**.
Listen to the different sounds of **ough** that you hear.

thorough	although	thought
dough	ought	brought
coughing	fought	doughnut

B. Use the words above to fill in the chart.

Long *o* sound as in *though*	Short *o* sound as in *cough*

160 Vowel Digraphs and Other Letter Combinations
Phonics

Practice It!

letter combinations
sounds of **ough**

What's Missing?

A. Read each word out loud. Circle the letters **ough**.

thought	dough	cough	bought	thorough
though	although	brought	doughnut	ought

B. Write a letter or letters to form words from above that complete the sentences. Read the sentences out loud.

1. Eric __ __ough__ a lot about his future.

2. I like thin pizza __ough, but Nelly likes thick.

3. Dogs can have a __ough, just like people.

4. I want to learn to speak Spanish, even __ __ough it will be hard.

5. Micah __ __ough__ her poster collection to class.

6. Dad did a __ __ __ __ough job of cleaning before the party started.

7. My __ough__ __ __ has grape jelly inside.

8. Mrs. Higgens __ough__ a round-trip ticket to New York City.

Review It!

letter combinations
sounds of **ough**

Name _____

Fill in the circle by the word that best completes each sentence.

Stop That Cough!

1. Kevin had a bad cold and had been _____ for days.
   - Ⓐ roughing
   - Ⓑ coughed
   - Ⓒ coughing

2. His dad _____ the doctor's advice.
   - Ⓐ sought
   - Ⓑ brought
   - Ⓒ though

3. The doctor gave Kevin a _____ exam.
   - Ⓐ thought
   - Ⓑ thorough
   - Ⓒ through

4. He _____ Kevin should rest, drink liquids, and eat chicken soup.
   - Ⓐ thought
   - Ⓑ through
   - Ⓒ although

5. "You _____ to feel better in a few days," the doctor said.
   - Ⓐ sought
   - Ⓑ brought
   - Ⓒ ought

6. Kevin stayed home, even _____ he wanted to go to school.
   - Ⓐ thoughtful
   - Ⓑ dough
   - Ⓒ though

7. By the third day, Kevin's _____ was almost gone.
   - Ⓐ though
   - Ⓑ tough
   - Ⓒ cough

8. His dad said, "You can go to school today, _____ I want you to take it easy."
   - Ⓐ through
   - Ⓑ although
   - Ⓒ rough

Foolproof Cooking

Read It!
variant vowel digraphs;
letter combinations

Ryan hated being the middle kid. His older brother, Moose, was cool. Moose was good-looking. Moose was the captain of the high school football team. Girls drooled over Moose like cats over tuna. People would say to Ryan, "You don't look like Moose."

Being Brooke's brother was tough, too. Brooke had won the Golden Pencil Award. Her drawing was a cartoon of a baboon family. She was the first child ever to win. People would say to Ryan, "You sure don't draw like your sister!"

Ryan wanted to be noticed, too. He decided to try cooking. "Cooking isn't tough," he thought. "All you need to do is follow the directions."

Ryan took a cookbook from the bookshelf. The title sounded perfect: *Foolproof Cooking.* He flipped through the pages. He decided to make a cake.

Ryan lined up spoons and bowls. He scooped and mixed. He worked at lightning speed. Then Ryan poured the dough into pans. His gloomy mood started to lift.

That night, Mom brought Ryan's cake to the table. She said, "Your cake looks too good to eat."

Ryan smiled as Moose said, "Cut me a big slice!" Moose took a big bite. He gagged.

Dad said, "Stop goofing around!"

Then Dad took a taste. He coughed and reached for his water. Mom tried a tiny bite. "It's salty!" she said.

"Oops! I must have used salt instead of sugar!" said Ryan. He felt stupid. His shoulders drooped.

"Hey, Ryan," said Moose. "I could never make a cake that looked this good."

Ryan smiled. "I bet next time sugar will make it *taste* good, too!"

Apply It!

variant vowel digraphs;
letter combinations

Name _____

Now Try This...

1. Look back at the story. Write four words for each sound.

oo sound as in *wood*	oo sound as in *cool*

2. Write a word from the story that has a long *o* sound spelled *ough*. _____

   Write a word from the story that has a short *o* sound spelled *ough*. _____

3. What could be a reason why Ryan used salt instead of sugar?

   _____

   _____

4. Could you understand why Ryan hated being the middle child? Explain your answer.

   _____

   _____

5. Why did Ryan think the cookbook he chose was perfect?

   _____

   _____

6. Practice reading two long paragraphs in the story. Then read them to your teacher.

R-Controlled Vowels

Overview
The purpose of the *R*-Controlled Vowels section is to help students decode words in which the *r* controls, or affects, the sound of the vowel that precedes it. Although students will probably be able to read simple one-syllable words that have *r*-controlled vowels, struggling readers may have more difficulty decoding longer, unfamiliar words.

Teaching Tips
You may want to use the following techniques to introduce the concepts in this section:

R-Controlled Vowels *pages 167–171*
- Write the following words on the board:

    part, herd, bird, for, burn

    Say each word, emphasizing the *r*-controlled vowel sound. Ask students to read each word out loud and to circle the vowel and the *r*.

- Ask students to compare the vowel sounds in the words on the board. Lead students to find the three words that have the /**ur**/ sound (*herd, bird,* and *burn*). Help students draw the conclusion that **er**, **ir**, and **ur** are different ways to spell the /**ur**/ sound.

Rule Breakers
When an *r*-controlled vowel appears in an unstressed syllable, it usually has the schwa + *r* sound. Students will learn about the schwa on pages 207–217. The only difference between the schwa + *r* sound and the /**ur**/ sound spelled **er**, **ir**, or **ur** is if the syllable is stressed. Students need not be able to differentiate between those two patterns. They need only to recognize the sounds represented by particular spellings in order to decode the words.

Pretest

r-controlled vowels
ar, or, er, ir, ur

Name _____

Read the first word in each row. Fill in the circle by the word that has the same sound as the underlined letters.

1. ch<u>ar</u>t	Ⓐ March	Ⓑ spare	Ⓒ scare
2. g<u>ar</u>den	Ⓐ area	Ⓑ dart	Ⓒ pear
3. n<u>or</u>th	Ⓐ flavor	Ⓑ storm	Ⓒ author
4. p<u>or</u>ch	Ⓐ corn	Ⓑ favor	Ⓒ labor
5. v<u>er</u>b	Ⓐ where	Ⓑ erase	Ⓒ herd
6. cl<u>er</u>k	Ⓐ terror	Ⓑ perfect	Ⓒ berry
7. st<u>ir</u>	Ⓐ fire	Ⓑ admire	Ⓒ dirty
8. c<u>ir</u>cle	Ⓐ shirt	Ⓑ tired	Ⓒ wire
9. b<u>ur</u>ning	Ⓐ sure	Ⓑ purse	Ⓒ crush
10. h<u>ur</u>t	Ⓐ curl	Ⓑ your	Ⓒ bury

Learn It!
r-controlled vowels

Name _____

ar, or, er, ir, ur

When a vowel is followed by the letter *r*, the *r* controls, or changes, the sound of the vowel.

Listen to the sounds of the *r*-controlled vowels in the words below. Notice that **er**, **ir**, and **ur** all have the same sound.

ar	or	er	ir	ur
M**ar**ch	f**or**ms	cl**er**k	st**ir**	t**ur**ns

A. Read each word out loud. Circle the vowel + *r* in each word.

serve	barked	third	chart	nerve
hurl	turkey	birth	perfect	storms
garden	swirl	porch	purse	forests

B. Use the words above to fill in the first three rows of the chart. Then add your own words to the last row.

ar as in March	or as in forms	er as in clerk	ir as in stir	ur as in turns

R-Controlled Vowels
Phonics

Practice It!
r-controlled vowels
ar, or, er, ir, ur

Name _____

What's the Word?

A. Read each word out loud. Circle the **r** + the vowel it controls.

| storm | germs | surf | skirts | snore |
| farms | purse | forests | birth | nerve |

B. Write a word from above that goes with the clue.

1. This is a bag not made of paper.   ___ ___ ___ ___ ___

2. Cows call these places home.   ___ ___ ___ ___ ___

3. These are small but mighty bugs.   ___ ___ ___ ___ ___

4. This is a way to ride a wave.   ___ ___ ___ ___

5. Girls can wear these short or long.   ___ ___ ___ ___ ___ ___

6. Deer call these places home.   ___ ___ ___ ___ ___ ___ ___

7. This can cause the power to go out.   ___ ___ ___ ___ ___

8. This is an event you celebrate every year. ___ ___ ___ ___ ___

C. Write a clue for the word *garden*.

_____

_____

_____

Review It!
r-controlled vowels
ar, or, er, ir, ur

Name _____

Fill in the circle by the word that best completes each sentence.

Don't Turn Your Back on a Purse

1. Ms. Burns knew she had placed her _____ on the floor next to a lamp.
   - Ⓐ perch
   - Ⓑ purse
   - Ⓒ perk

2. She had put down her purse before giving a _____ gift to Mrs. Fort.
   - Ⓐ burning
   - Ⓑ birth
   - Ⓒ birthday

3. "I'm _____ that I left my purse on the floor," Ms. Burns said to Mrs. Marks.
   - Ⓐ curtain
   - Ⓑ certain
   - Ⓒ circle

4. "I wonder where my purse is," Mrs. Marks said as she _____ looking around.
   - Ⓐ parted
   - Ⓑ darted
   - Ⓒ started

5. "Well, that's the _____ purse to go missing," said Ms. Stern.
   - Ⓐ thirst
   - Ⓑ thirteen
   - Ⓒ third

6. "Mine isn't on the _____ where I left it," she added.
   - Ⓐ porch
   - Ⓑ perch
   - Ⓒ pork

7. Suddenly, the women heard sharp _____ coming from the next room.
   - Ⓐ barking
   - Ⓑ marking
   - Ⓒ reporting

8. There they saw Mrs. Fort's puppy, sitting on a _____ pile of purses!
   - Ⓐ lard
   - Ⓑ large
   - Ⓒ lark

Read It!
r-controlled vowels

A POWERFUL PUNCH!

A soft breeze can lift a leaf and make it dance. A forceful wind can lift a car and hurl it. A tornado is a powerful wind that takes the form of a very dark cloud. The cloud is shaped like a funnel. Because it swirls and spins, a tornado is known as a twister.

Tornadoes are said to be one of nature's most fierce storms. Some twisters are stronger than others. The strongest tornadoes have the fastest winds. They cause the most harm.

Some tornadoes break branches off trees. Others grab forests right out of the ground. Some tornadoes peel off roofs. Others shatter homes in seconds.

A large number of tornadoes can occur in a short time. On April 3 and 4, 1974, a super outburst of tornadoes hit the country. It was reported that 148 twisters struck thirteen states. The tornadoes killed more than 300 people. They injured more than 5,000 others.

Some people think that places near rivers, seas, and lakes are safe from tornadoes. That is not correct. In fact, tornadoes do form over water. Those tornadoes are called waterspouts.

A waterspout is weaker than most land tornadoes. But it is dangerous. A waterspout can overturn boats and wreck ships. If a waterspout whirls ashore, it is called a tornado.

In the United States, people report about 800 tornadoes a year. These storms cause injuries and sometimes deaths. They cause a lot of damage. Tornadoes pack a powerful punch!

Apply It!
r-controlled vowels

Name _____

Now Try This...

1. Look back at the story. Write three words for each sound.

ar as in *March*			
or as in *forms*			
er as in *germ*			
ir as in *stir*			
ur as in *turns*			

2. What could be one reason that tornadoes cause a lot of damage?

   _____

   _____

3. How is a waterspout different from a tornado?

   _____

   _____

4. Think about all you know about tornadoes. Do you agree with people who say tornadoes are nature's most fierce storms? Explain your answer.

   _____

   _____

   _____

5. Practice reading two paragraphs in the story. Then read them to your teacher.

Silent Consonants

Overview
The purpose of the **Silent Consonants** section is to help students recognize letter patterns that often signal a silent letter. Learning these patterns will minimize the frustration struggling readers experience when they encounter words that break the rules they have already internalized about letter/sound relationships.

Teaching Tips
You may want to use the following techniques to introduce the concepts in this section:

Silent Consonant Patterns *pages 174–187*
- Write the following words on the board:

    lamb, know, wrist, sign, science, soften, half

    Cover the silent letter in each word with a sticky-backed paper, and then have students sound out the word.
- Write the following words on the board:

    hour, chalk, listen, comb, wrong, knife, gnat

    Read the words out loud. Invite volunteers to cross out the silent letter in each word.

Rule Breakers
Silent letters occur in words for two reasons: 1) the pronunciation has changed over time, but the spelling has not (for example, the **k** in *know* was once pronounced); or 2) the word is borrowed from another language (for example, the **t** is silent in the French word *ballet*).

Since brain research has shown that the brain detects patterns, a useful strategy for students to use when decoding a word is to think of a familiar word with the same letter pattern. For example, to decode the unfamiliar word *wrath,* the student could recall words beginning with **wr** and conclude that the **w** will not be pronounced.

Pretest
silent consonants

Name _____

Read each word out loud. Cross out the silent consonant, the consonant you do not hear.

1. half
2. rhyme
3. often
4. climb
5. knob
6. gnat
7. scene
8. wrapped

9. doubt
10. listen
11. walk
12. fasten
13. knee
14. thumb
15. sign
16. scent

Silent Consonants
Phonics

Learn It!
silent consonants

Name _____

Silent *h* and Silent *l*

Sometimes one or more letters in a word are not sounded. These letters are called *silent letters*.

Read the words below and notice that the *h* and the *l* are not said.

herb   ca**l**f

A. Read each word out loud. Cross out the **silent h** or the **silent l**. Read each word again.

~~h~~our	talk	oh	honest
yolk	Thomas	chalk	rhino
honor	folks	walk	half

B. Use the words above to fill in the chart.

Silent *h*	Silent *l*

Practice It!
silent consonants
h, l

Name _____

Crossword Time!

A. Read each word out loud. Cross out the silent letter.

| herb | chalk | ghost | stalks | rhyme |
| salmon | honor | yolk | rhino | folks |

B. Use words above to complete the crossword puzzle.

Across

1. a soft rock used for writing
4. a large animal with a horn on its nose
7. the yellow part of an egg
8. a large fish used for food

Down

2. a plant used in cooking
3. people
5. parts of plants where the leaves grow
6. to give praise or an award

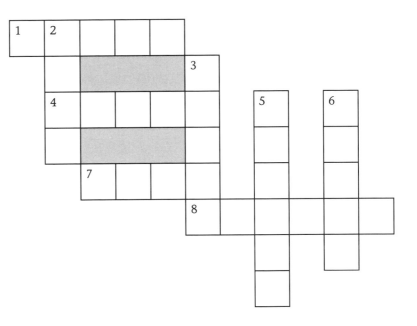

Silent Consonants
Phonics
175

Name _____

Review It!
silent consonants
h, l

Fill in the circle by the word that best completes each sentence.

The County Fair

1. A lot of _____ entered contests in this year's county fair.
   - Ⓐ folks
   - Ⓑ yolks
   - Ⓒ salmon

2. My grandfather hoped to win first prize for a _____ he showed.
   - Ⓐ talk
   - Ⓑ half
   - Ⓒ calf

3. I brought tall _____ of bright yellow sunflowers.
   - Ⓐ chalks
   - Ⓑ stalks
   - Ⓒ herbs

4. Eggs with double _____ were an odd entry.
   - Ⓐ folks
   - Ⓑ rhymes
   - Ⓒ yolks

5. Younger kids made drawings with _____ and hung them on a wall.
   - Ⓐ chalk
   - Ⓑ rhinos
   - Ⓒ stalks

6. My sister stitched a _____ on cloth and framed it, too.
   - Ⓐ half
   - Ⓑ rhyme
   - Ⓒ walk

7. The judges worked for _____ checking each entry.
   - Ⓐ honest
   - Ⓑ hours
   - Ⓒ halves

8. People knew it was an _____ to be an award winner!
   - Ⓐ hour
   - Ⓑ honest
   - Ⓒ honor

Learn It!
silent consonants

Name _____

Silent *t* and Silent *c*

The consonant *t* is often silent after *s*.   fasten
The *t* can be silent in other words, too.   often
The consonant *c* can be silent after *s*.   scent

A. Read each word out loud. Cross out the silent *t* or the silent *c*. Read each word again.

cas~~t~~le	scent	scented	soften
listen	scissors	glisten	scene
whistle	science	scientist	fasten

B. Use the words above to fill in the chart.

Silent *t*	Silent *c*

Silent Consonants
Phonics
177

Practice It!
silent consonants
t, c

Name _____

What Am I?

A. Read each word out loud. Cross out the silent letter.

fasten   scent   whistle   glistens   castle

science   scientist   listening   scenery   scissors

B. Draw lines to match the clues and the words.

1. I am given off by a flower.   a. listening
2. I am a tool used to cut.   b. scenery
3. I am a home to kings and queens.   c. scientist
4. I am a way snow sparkles.   d. scent
5. I am the background used in a play.   e. whistle
6. I am an action done with ears.   f. glistens
7. I am the study of nature.   g. scissors
8. I am a person who studies nature.   h. fasten
9. I am what you do to a seat belt.   i. castle
10. I am used to make a loud sound.   j. science

C. Write an "I am" clue for *science fiction*.

I am _____

_____

Review It!
silent consonants
t, c

Name _____

Fill in the circle by the word that best completes each sentence.

Scenery and Sets

1. Our class put on a play that had two acts and three _____.
   - Ⓐ scents
   - Ⓑ sciences
   - Ⓒ scenes

2. The play took place in a _____ during the Middle Ages.
   - Ⓐ castle
   - Ⓑ wrestle
   - Ⓒ scene

3. I was on the crew that built the _____.
   - Ⓐ whistles
   - Ⓑ scenery
   - Ⓒ scenes

4. We _____ carefully as our teacher explained how to use the tools.
   - Ⓐ listened
   - Ⓑ fastened
   - Ⓒ softened

5. We _____ tall towers with hinges so that they would unfold.
   - Ⓐ listened
   - Ⓑ wrestled
   - Ⓒ fastened

6. The towers were sturdy, so two guys could not knock them down in a _____ scene.
   - Ⓐ wrestling
   - Ⓑ fastening
   - Ⓒ honoring

7. As a backdrop, we painted a night sky with stars that _____.
   - Ⓐ listened
   - Ⓑ wrapped
   - Ⓒ glistened

8. After working all weekend, my arm _____ ached!
   - Ⓐ castles
   - Ⓑ scissors
   - Ⓒ muscles

Learn It!
silent consonants

Name _____

Silent g and Silent k

The consonants **g** and **k** are often silent before **n**.

Read the words below and notice that the **g** and the **k** are not said.

gnaw **k**nob

A. Read each word out loud. Cross out the silent **g** or the silent **k**. Read each word again.

~~k~~neel   gnome   knob   knit

gnat   knock   sign   design

knot   assign   knack   gnash

B. Use the words above to fill in the chart.

Silent g	Silent k

Practice It!
silent consonants
g, k

Name _____

Silent Letter Scramble

A. Read each word out loud. Cross out the silent letter.

kneecap	sign	knuckle	knots	design
knock	gnat	assign	gnash	kneel

B. Read each clue. Then unscramble the answer and write it on the lines.

1. to get down on your knees — elken
2. they keep shoelaces tied — tnoks
3. to give homework to — gnassi
4. a tiny bug that bites — tang
5. the bone covering your knee — eenkpac
6. a plan — desing
7. to rap your knuckles on a door — konck
8. to write your name on a paper — ngis

C. Unscramble the circled letters above to answer the clue.

They kept their clothes shiny.

___ ___ ___ ___ h ___ ___

Review It!
silent consonants
g, *k*

Name _____

Fill in the circle by the word that best completes each sentence.

A Good-Luck Sign

1. I was deep into a book when I heard a loud _____ at the door.

    Ⓐ knot   Ⓑ knew   Ⓒ knock

2. I _____ just who it was.

    Ⓐ knew   Ⓑ knotted   Ⓒ knit

3. Uncle Knute stood on the porch holding a little _____ made of stone.

    Ⓐ kneecap   Ⓑ gnome   Ⓒ knot

4. "I _____ you are planting a garden, so I brought you this," said Uncle Knute.

    Ⓐ known   Ⓑ know   Ⓒ knead

5. "This gnome is _____ to have special powers," he said with a wink.

    Ⓐ known   Ⓑ gnawed   Ⓒ know

6. I liked the gnome's _____ because he sat reading a book.

    Ⓐ sign   Ⓑ design   Ⓒ assign

7. "Thanks, Uncle Knute. You have a _____ for buying me great gifts," I said.

    Ⓐ knob   Ⓑ knack   Ⓒ gnat

8. "I think I'll put the gnome next to the _____ that says *Jackie's Garden*," I added.

    Ⓐ knuckle   Ⓑ sign   Ⓒ assign

Learn It!
silent consonants

Name _____

Silent *b* and Silent *w*

The consonant *b* is often silent after *m*.   crumb
The *b* also can be silent before *t*.   debt
The consonant *w* is often silent before *r*.   wrap

A. Read each word out loud. Cross out the silent *b* or the silent *w*. Read each word again.

~~w~~reck	comb	wring	writing
thumb	wrong	limb	wrist
numb	lamb	answer	doubt

B. Use the words above to fill in the chart.

Silent *b*	Silent *w*

Silent Consonants
Phonics

Practice It!
silent consonants
b, w

Name _____

Answer These Riddles!

A. Read each word out loud. Cross out the silent letter.

| wrapper | wrong | plumber | limbs | wrist |
| wrinkle | thumb | answer | doubt | crumb |

B. Use the words above to answer the riddles.

1. I hang around candy. _____

2. I am never sure. _____

3. Put me up to say it's okay. _____

4. Every question wants me. _____

5. I am never right. _____

6. We're also known as arms and legs. _____

7. I wear a watch. _____

8. An iron makes me go away. _____

C. Write a riddle for the word *wreath*.

_____

_____

_____.

Review It!
silent consonants
b, w

Name _____

Fill in the circle by the word that best completes each sentence.

A Storm to Write About

1. I have no _____ that this snowstorm is the worst on record.
   - Ⓐ debt
   - Ⓑ thumb
   - Ⓒ doubt

2. Tree _____ snapped from the heavy ice.
   - Ⓐ thumbs
   - Ⓑ limbs
   - Ⓒ combs

3. We had to _____ over the snow to get out the door.
   - Ⓐ climb
   - Ⓑ wring
   - Ⓒ write

4. Our fingers were _____ after hours of shoveling.
   - Ⓐ wrong
   - Ⓑ thumbs
   - Ⓒ numb

5. The pipes froze and burst, so Dad tried to reach a _____.
   - Ⓐ plumb
   - Ⓑ plumber
   - Ⓒ wrestler

6. Plumbers were busy and didn't _____ Dad's call for an hour.
   - Ⓐ answer
   - Ⓑ write
   - Ⓒ wrinkle

7. The water had made a _____ of our basement.
   - Ⓐ wrapper
   - Ⓑ wrist
   - Ⓒ wreck

8. We wore gloves when we had to _____ out the area rugs.
   - Ⓐ limb
   - Ⓑ wring
   - Ⓒ write

Read It!
silent consonants

Why Did You Sign Me Up for Camp?

"I can't believe I'm at this dumb camp," whined Carlos. His parents had signed him up for three weeks! So far, he had been at camp for two days. Carlos hated every minute.

On their first day, the campers swam in Knob Lake. Carlos thought the bottom felt like muddy slime. Then something cold bit at his knee. Carlos yelled. A camper named Cody told him not to worry. It was just a fish.

The boys played softball the next day. The ball socked Carlos in the wrist and made it numb. A nurse wrapped his wrist in a bandage that stretched. She fastened it with a metal clip.

Now it was the third day, and everyone was on a hike. Stalks of thorny twigs scratched Carlos. They felt as sharp as scissors. The stinky scent of skunk filled the air. Packs of gnats bit and stung. Carlos wished he were at home.

Finally, the boys began climbing a ridge. Carlos lagged behind. At last they reached the top. "It's nothing but stones," thought Carlos. Then he peeked over the edge. He had never been so high up. The camp lay far below. It looked like a toy! The scene amazed him.

Cody let out a low whistle. Then he walked over to Carlos. The boys stood quietly. Carlos spotted a bird circling above. He nudged Cody. "Check out the red-tailed hawk," said Carlos.

"Whoa!" answered Cody. "I didn't know that was a hawk."

Carlos had aching calf muscles. But he felt that he may have been wrong. Camp might not be such a dumb place after all.

Apply It!
silent consonants

Name _____

Now Try This...

1. Look back at the story. Write three words for each silent letter.

c	b	w

2. Write two words from the story that have the silent letter *l*.

   _____   _____

3. Describe how you would feel if you were Carlos during his first two days at camp. Tell why you would feel that way.

   _____
   _____
   _____

4. Write two words that describe Carlos before the hike.

   _____   _____

5. Write two clues that tell you Cody and Carlos probably will be friends.

   _____
   _____

6. Practice reading two paragraphs in the story. Then read them to your teacher.

Diphthongs

Overview
The purpose of the **Diphthongs** section is to help students read words that have a diphthong, or a sound formed by saying two vowel sounds quickly together. This section covers two diphthongs: /**oi**/ (as in *boil, boy*) and /**ow**/ (as in *found, crown*).

Teaching Tips
You may want to use the following techniques to introduce the concepts in this section:

Diphthongs *pages 190–195*
- To practice decoding words that have diphthongs, have students suggest rhyming words for *boy* and *oil*. If needed, give students clues, such as:

    What is a word that means "to bother or bug"? (annoy)

    What is a word that means "to heat until it bubbles"? (boil)

    What is a word that means "a loud sound"? (noise)

    What is a word that means "to have a good time"? (enjoy)

    Invite a student to write each suggested rhyming word on the board. Then have students circle the diphthong in each word.

- Repeat the entire process above with *down* and *cloud*. Give clues, such as:

    What is a word that means "a performer at a circus"? (clown)

    What is a word that means "to say in a loud voice"? (shout)

    What is a word that means "to name numbers in order"? (count)

    What is a word that means "a place to live that's smaller than a city"? (town)

Rule Breakers
You may call students' attention to additional pronunciations of letter pairs *ou* and *ow*. For example, listen to the sounds of *ou* and *ow* in the following words: *soup, touch, grow*.

Pretest
diphthongs

Name _____

A. Fill in the circle next to the word in each row that has the /**oi**/ sound as in *boil*.

1. Ⓐ tool Ⓑ toil Ⓒ toll Ⓓ troll

2. Ⓐ hold Ⓑ party Ⓒ stole Ⓓ broil

3. Ⓐ story Ⓑ destroy Ⓒ football Ⓓ pony

4. Ⓐ point Ⓑ brown Ⓒ trolley Ⓓ buys

5. Ⓐ boots Ⓑ bride Ⓒ annoy Ⓓ body

6. Ⓐ enjoy Ⓑ empty Ⓒ jolly Ⓓ jumpy

B. Fill in the circle next to the word in each row that has the /**ow**/ sound as in *down*.

1. Ⓐ show Ⓑ flow Ⓒ cough Ⓓ bounce

2. Ⓐ although Ⓑ clown Ⓒ know Ⓓ sunny

3. Ⓐ shown Ⓑ shone Ⓒ shout Ⓓ solid

4. Ⓐ boots Ⓑ lunch Ⓒ product Ⓓ proud

5. Ⓐ allow Ⓑ groan Ⓒ grown Ⓓ group

6. Ⓐ circle Ⓑ enough Ⓒ somehow Ⓓ dough

Learn It!
diphthongs

Name _____

oi, oy

A diphthong is a vowel pair in which two sounds slide together and have a new sound. The vowel pairs **oi** and **oy** both have the same sound of **/oi/**.

Listen for the sound of **/oi/** in these words:

b**oi**l   b**oy**

A. Read each word out loud. Circle the vowel pairs that spell the **/oi/** sound.

broil	destroy	point	toys
enjoy	spoil	joyful	annoy
avoid	joined	loyal	noise

B. Write in words from above. Then add your own words to the last row.

/oi/ sound spelled *oi*	/oi/ sound spelled *oy*

Diphthongs
Phonics

Learn It!
diphthongs

Name _____

ou, ow

A diphthong is a vowel pair in which two sounds slide together and have a new sound. The vowel pairs **ou** and **ow** both have the same sound of **/ow/**.

Listen for the sound of **/ow/** in these words:

                f**ou**nd   cr**ow**d

A. Read each word out loud. Circle the letters that spell the **/ow/** sound.

gown	downtown	scout	eyebrow
doubt	shout	somehow	growl
amount	drown	bound	cloud

B. Write in words from above. Then add your own words to the last row.

/ow/ sound spelled **ow**	/ow/ sound spelled **ou**

Diphthongs

Phonics

Practice It!
diphthongs
oi/oy; ou/ow

Name _____

Find Those Words!

A. Read each word out loud. Circle the letters that spell the **/oi/** sound. Underline the letters that spell the **/ow/** sound.

count	drown	moist	noisy	bounded
annoy	growl	town	somehow	employ

B. Circle the words above in the puzzle. The words can read down, across, or diagonally.

```
O D A B S O M E H O W
N M O N E M P L O Y E
D O O W N A N N O Y I
M N I I N O M N M T O
B N Y S S S I N I O S
O E S E Y T O C Y O M
U D G P G N S M O W O
N R R L R O T N E N I
D O O O W O W A D H S
E W W Y U O C I N T O
D N L E T C O U N T U
```

C. Write nine of the words you circled.

_____ _____ _____

_____ _____ _____

_____ _____ _____

Diphthongs
Phonics

Review It!

diphthongs
oi/oy; ou/ow

Name _____

Fill in the circle by the word that best completes each sentence.

Avoiding the Clowns

1. The Browns loved the circus, so they got tickets when it came to _____.

    Ⓐ tower   Ⓑ town   Ⓒ frown

2. "I really _____ watching the acrobats," said Mom.

    Ⓐ employ   Ⓑ overjoy   Ⓒ enjoy

3. "How do tightrope walkers _____ looking down?" Roy asked.

    Ⓐ allow   Ⓑ avoid   Ⓒ annoy

4. "I _____ that they even think about falling," Dad said.

    Ⓐ doubt   Ⓑ down   Ⓒ spout

5. "Don't turn _____, but the clowns are heading our way," Howard said.

    Ⓐ allowed   Ⓑ crowds   Ⓒ around

6. "I think it's _____ when they honk their horns by your ears!" Roy said.

    Ⓐ destroying   Ⓑ annoying   Ⓒ spoiling

7. "I know how we can avoid their _____," Howard said.

    Ⓐ avoid   Ⓑ noise   Ⓒ soil

8. "I _____ some seats where the clowns won't be near us," Howard said. "Let's go."

    Ⓐ around   Ⓑ round   Ⓒ found

Read It!
diphthongs

Scout Gets Out!

"I'm home!" Troy shouted. He couldn't wait to show off the trout he had caught. Troy went to wrap the fish in foil and get it into the fridge.

Troy's mom stomped in from the yard. "Scout got out again!" Her voice sounded annoyed. "You better join in the search. Dad's gone that way!" She pointed down the street.

Scout was Troy's dog. Troy had locked Scout in the yard that morning. Somehow, Scout got out. No doubt, Scout was out prowling around.

Scout had gotten out just last week. He strayed downtown. The dog pound called hours later. Scout had wound up there. Dad had to pay to get Scout back. Dad was quite the grouch for the rest of the day.

Troy grabbed the chow that Scout liked best. Then he walked down the block and started calling the dog. There was no sign of Scout.

Troy stopped. Someone was grilling meat! Troy knew a hound dog like Scout would follow that scent.

Troy spotted a cloud of smoke. It floated from behind a brown house. He headed into the backyard. Troy found the meat. He also found Scout.

Scout was crouched low on the ground near the grill. A large steak was cooking on it. Scout's snout jiggled. His mouth drooled. Scout was about to pounce and grab some dinner!

Troy shouted, "Come here, Scout!" Troy showed Scout the chow.

Scout looked at Troy. Then he looked at the steak. He had to make a choice. Scout bounded toward Troy, howling.

"Good boy," said Troy. "Now let's go home and stay there."

Apply It!
diphthongs

Name _____

Now Try This...

1. Look back at the story. Write words for each of the sounds in the chart. The number in each box tells how many words to write.

/oi/ spelled *oi* (3)	
/oi/ spelled *oy* (2)	
/ou/ spelled *ou* (3)	
/ou/ spelled *ow* (3)	

2. Look at the last three paragraphs in the story. Circle nine different words that have the /**oi**/ or /**ou**/ sounds.

3. Why did Troy take chow when he went to look for Scout?

   _____

   _____

4. How do you know that Scout likes Troy?

   _____

   _____

5. What might Troy do to keep Scout from running away?

   _____

   _____

6. Practice reading two paragraphs in the story. Then read them to your teacher.

Syllable Patterns

Overview
The purpose of the **Syllable Patterns** section is to help students decode multisyllabic words by first breaking them into syllables, or units of pronunciation that have one vowel sound. Students then apply their knowledge of letter/sound relationships to each syllable.

Teaching Tips
You may want to use the following techniques to introduce the concepts in this section:

Syllables *pages 198–200*
Say each of the following words as you write it on the board: *candy, absent, sudden, wonderful, umbrella, cabin.* Now slowly repeat each word, and have students tap along with you as you emphasize each syllable. Write the number of syllables next to each word. Then say each word a third time, and tell students to raise their hands when they hear a vowel sound. Point out that each vowel sound is a syllable.

Double Consonants and Syllables *pages 201–205*
Write the following words on the board: *zipper, carry, hurry, lesson, mammal.* Ask what the words have in common (double middle consonants). Read the words out loud. Have students determine how many vowel sounds they hear in each word and, therefore, how many syllables each word has (two). Explain to students that words having a double consonant in the middle are usually divided between the consonants. Have volunteers divide the words into syllables.

Schwa Sound in Initial Syllables *pages 207–209*
Use the following words to review stressed and unstressed syllables: *rapid, until, zebra.* Read each word out loud and write **s** above the stressed syllable and **u** above the unstressed. Then have students do the same with the following words: *along, divide, compare, about.* Ask students to listen for the unstressed beginning sound (it sounds kind of like "uh") as you say the four words again. Write the word *schwa* on the board, and explain that it is the name for the vowel sound heard in an unstressed syllable.

Final Schwa + /n/, /l/, or /r/ *pages 210–217*
If necessary, review stressed and unstressed syllables, as well as the schwa sound, reusing the suggestions above. Then write these words on the board: *nickel, civil, table.* Point out the schwa + /l/ sound heard at the end of each word. Next write: *seven, lemon, robin.* Point out the schwa + /n/ sound at the end. Then explain that the schwa + /r/ sound is often heard at the end of a word, too. List examples, such as *favor, solar, tower.* Read the words out loud and have students repeat them.

Rule Breakers
Explain briefly to students that the schwa covers a range of sounds (such as /uh/, ĭ) and a range of spellings (such as, **ie** in *patient*, **y** in *oxygen*). Look through classroom dictionaries to see how the schwa sound is represented in the following words: *nickel, oxygen, dozen, adjust.*

Pretest

syllables;
syllable patterns

Name _____

A. Read the word. On the first line, write how many vowel sounds you hear.
On the second line, write how many syllables the word has.

1. magic   _____ vowel sounds   _____ syllables

2. camper   _____ vowel sounds   _____ syllables

3. season   _____ vowel sounds   _____ syllables

4. zipper   _____ vowel sounds   _____ syllables

5. screech   _____ vowel sounds   _____ syllables

6. tornado   _____ vowel sounds   _____ syllables

B. Read the word. Fill in the circle next to the correct way to divide the word into syllables.

1. captain   Ⓐ cap / ta / in   Ⓑ cap / tain

2. borrow   Ⓐ bo / rrow   Ⓑ bor / row

3. absent   Ⓐ ab / sent   Ⓑ abs / ent

4. favor   Ⓐ fa / vor   Ⓑ fav / or

5. hurry   Ⓐ hurr / y   Ⓑ hur / ry

6. final   Ⓐ fi / nal   Ⓑ fin / al

Syllable Patterns
Phonics
197

Name _____

Syllables

A syllable is a word part that has one vowel sound.
The number of vowel sounds in a word equals the number of syllables.

n<u>a</u>pk<u>i</u>n = 2 vowel sounds   m<u>u</u>lt<u>i</u>pl<u>y</u> = 3 vowel sounds

nap | kin = 2 syllables   mul | ti | ply = 3 syllables

A. Read each word out loud. Write the number of vowel sounds and the number of syllables you hear.

	Vowel Sounds	Syllables
sudden		
absent		
profile		
cabin		
cactus		
common		
moment		
subject		
habitat		
secret		

B. Fill in the missing syllables to make some of the words above.

mo_____   _____den   com_____   _____sent

cac_____   _____file   cab_____   hab___tat

198 Syllable Patterns
Phonics   Phonics and Word Study • EMC 3361 • © Evan-Moor Corp.

Practice It!
syllable patterns

Name _____

Dividing Words
Many words are divided into syllables, or parts, in these ways:
- Between consonants

    sub | ject   rib | bon

- Between a consonant and a vowel

    If the first vowel sound is long, divide the word after the long vowel.

    fi | nal

    If the first vowel sound is short, divide the word after the consonant.

    hab | it

A. Read each word out loud. Draw a long line to divide it into syllables.

cabin   medal   China   velvet   office

practice   local   atlas   spider   absent

B. Match the syllables to form a word above. Then write the word on the line.

1. of   a. al   _____

2. lo   b. vet   _____

3. med   c. las   _____

4. Chi   d. fice   office

5. ab   e. cal   _____

6. vel   f. sent   _____

7. spi   g. na   _____

8. at   h. der   _____

Review It!
multisyllabic words

Name _____

Fill in the circle by the word that best completes each sentence.

Band Practice

1. My favorite _____ at school is English, but I love to play in the band, too.
   - Ⓐ submit
   - Ⓑ subject
   - Ⓒ subtract

2. I go to band _____ every Monday and Wednesday.
   - Ⓐ proper
   - Ⓑ problem
   - Ⓒ practice

3. Mr. Mason, our bandleader, doesn't like kids to be _____ from practice.
   - Ⓐ absent
   - Ⓑ admit
   - Ⓒ addition

4. He says there is a _____ between practicing a lot and playing well.
   - Ⓐ condition
   - Ⓑ continent
   - Ⓒ connection

5. I think he expects us to win music awards and _____.
   - Ⓐ metals
   - Ⓑ magnets
   - Ⓒ medals

6. Mr. Mason says he wants us to _____ well when we play.
   - Ⓐ perform
   - Ⓑ profile
   - Ⓒ permit

7. No one is a _____ fan of the band than Mr. Mason.
   - Ⓐ beggar
   - Ⓑ bigger
   - Ⓒ biggest

8. At our concerts, it is no _____ that he is proud of us.
   - Ⓐ season
   - Ⓑ stuffing
   - Ⓒ secret

Learn It!
syllable patterns

Name _____

Double Consonants and Syllables

Words that have a double consonant in the middle are usually divided between the two consonants.

mid | dle   hur | ry

A. Read each word out loud. Draw a long line to divide the word into syllables.

platter   hurried   clapping   carry

puddle   zipper   litter   pillow

fellow   humming   buddy   common

B. Fill in the missing double *d*, *g*, *l*, or *p* to form common words. Then draw a line to divide each word into syllables.

1. pa___ ___le

2. sha___ ___ow

3. sli___ ___er

4. hi___ ___en

5. ru___ ___ed

6. pe___ ___er

7. gi___ ___le

8. vi___ ___age

Syllable Patterns
Phonics

Practice It!
syllable patterns
double consonants

Name _____

Double Consonant Scramble

A. Read each word out loud. Draw a long line to divide the word into syllables.

| butter | paddle | mammals | shopping | happy |
| follows | fossil | running | puddles | humming |

B. Read the clue. Then unscramble the answer and write it on the lines.

1. an action needing bags or carts   pinghops   __ __ __ __ __Ⓞ__
2. what heavy rains leave behind   pedulds   __ __ __Ⓞ__ __
3. their babies are born live   amlamsm   __ __ __ __ __ __ __
4. this is used to move a small boat   dapled   __ __Ⓞ__ __ __
5. a fat that melts on toast   tubert   __ __ __ __Ⓞ__
6. a seashell turned into stone   osfils   __ __ __ __ __Ⓞ
7. what April does to March   loflows   __ __ __ __ __ __ __
8. singing with your mouth closed   mumingh   __Ⓞ__ __ __ __

C. Unscramble the circled letters above to fill in the answer.

The double consonants in the words above appear

in the __ __ __ __ __ __.

Review It!

syllable patterns
double consonants

Name _____

Fill in the circle by the word that best completes each sentence.

Shopping for Running Shoes

1. Han and his family were _____ at the outdoor mall.
   - Ⓐ mopping
   - Ⓑ hopping
   - Ⓒ shopping

2. Han needed _____ shoes for track.
   - Ⓐ running
   - Ⓑ wrapping
   - Ⓒ sunning

3. His last pair was ruined after he had stepped in a deep _____.
   - Ⓐ paddle
   - Ⓑ huddle
   - Ⓒ puddle

4. Han's mother _____ his baby sister while they shopped.
   - Ⓐ huddled
   - Ⓑ carried
   - Ⓒ collected

5. "Just _____ me so you don't get lost," Mrs. Pham said to Han and his brothers.
   - Ⓐ narrow
   - Ⓑ borrow
   - Ⓒ follow

6. Han was _____ to be getting new running shoes, so he stayed close to his mom.
   - Ⓐ happy
   - Ⓑ groggy
   - Ⓒ sappy

7. When Han saw the shoe store, he _____ over to see what styles there were.
   - Ⓐ hammered
   - Ⓑ hurried
   - Ⓒ married

8. "These shoes are _____ than my old ones!" Han said as he tried on a pair.
   - Ⓐ butter
   - Ⓑ letter
   - Ⓒ better

KLUE, Secret Agent

The stone wall was too rugged to climb. But that didn't worry Klue. He simply waved his hand. The ring he wore looked like a lion's head. A beam of light shone from the lion's open mouth. The beam lit up a hidden rock.

Klue twisted the rock. The wall slid open. He saw two women standing in an office. Amy Kwan was a scientist who did secret underwater research. Admiral Eva Ramos stood beside Kwan.

Klue stepped inside. The stone wall closed quietly behind him. He noticed that the wall was a bookcase on the inside. He wondered how the bookcase opened. A secret agent like Klue liked to solve these puzzles.

"Klue, get in here," said Kwan. "We have a terrible situation."

"We need you to fly to Morocco," said the Admiral. "Our plans for a sea lab are missing. We think a double agent stole them. It's vital that you recover the plans."

"You can rely on me," said Klue.

"Good! You'll need this device," said Kwan. She held up a yellow spider on a chain. "Press the spider's head to trigger a laser. It will cut through anything. Carry it at all times."

"I'll take that!" hissed Admiral Ramos. She grabbed the chain and slipped on a gas mask. At the same time, a cloud of gas burst from the medals on her jacket.

"Get her!" said Amy. She could hardly breathe. "Ramos must be the spy!"

"I've got to get out of here!" thought Klue. He tried to reach the bookcase, but his arms couldn't move.

Suddenly, a cold hand grabbed his shoulder. "Luke! You've tangled yourself in the sheets!" Luke's brother Eddie stood near his bed. "We have to get to our swimming lessons."

It was time to be Luke, regular guy.

Apply It!
syllable patterns

Name _____

Now Try This...

1. Look back at the story. List six words and divide each one into syllables.

Words with double consonants in the middle	

2. Draw a long line to divide each word into syllables.

    device   agent   laser   office   wondered

3. What secret underwater research might Amy be doing?

_____

_____

4. Why do you think Admiral Ramos wanted the yellow spider?

_____

_____

5. Why couldn't Luke move his arms?

_____

6. Practice reading two paragraphs in the story. Then read them to your teacher.

Pretest

syllables; schwa

Name _____

A. Read each word. Look at its two syllables. Circle the stressed, or emphasized, syllable. Underline the syllable that is not stressed.

1. alone
   a | lone

2. cactus
   cac | tus

3. combine
   com | bine

4. profile
   pro | file

5. common
   com | mon

6. police
   po | lice

B. Read each row of words. Fill in the circle next to the word that **begins** with the schwa, or **/uh/**, sound.

1. Ⓐ party Ⓑ potato Ⓒ velvet Ⓓ simple

2. Ⓐ goblet Ⓑ cable Ⓒ afraid Ⓓ robin

3. Ⓐ aloud Ⓑ lemon Ⓒ pillow Ⓓ limit

4. Ⓐ chapter Ⓑ manner Ⓒ outbreak Ⓓ complete

C. Read each row of words. Fill in the circle next to the word that **ends** with the same schwa + **/l/** sound you hear at the end of *pencil*.

1. Ⓐ refill Ⓑ landing Ⓒ until Ⓓ sample

2. Ⓐ normal Ⓑ retell Ⓒ speller Ⓓ lily

D. Read each row of words. Fill in the circle next to the word that **ends** with the same schwa + **/n/** sound you hear at the end of *season*.

1. Ⓐ snow Ⓑ happen Ⓒ unknown Ⓓ liner

2. Ⓐ begin Ⓑ than Ⓒ oven Ⓓ frosty

Syllable Patterns
Phonics

Learn It!
unstressed syllables

Name _____

The Schwa Sound

When a word has more than one syllable, one syllable is stressed, or emphasized, and the other syllable or syllables are unstressed. The vowel in an unstressed syllable often has the schwa sound. The schwa can sound like /uh/ and is shown as ə in a dictionary.

Listen for the schwa sound in these words:

robin	candle	instant
rob | **ən**	can | **dəl**	in | **stənt**

Some words begin with an unstressed syllable.
Listen for the schwa sound in the first syllable of these words:

parade	afraid
pə | rade	**ə** | fraid

A. Read each word out loud. Listen for the schwa sound in the unstressed first syllable.

about	against	alert	potato
ahead	divide	pollute	compare
correct	division	describe	pajamas

B. When the schwa is heard in the first syllable, you usually divide after the schwa sound. Draw a long line to divide each word into syllables.

| alert | about | above | ahead | aloud |
| divide | police | afraid | degree | against |

Practice It!
unstressed syllables
initial schwa

Name _____

Match Up

A. Read each word out loud. Circle the unstressed first syllable.

| against | alone | combine | correct | degree |
| pajamas | potato | divide | polite | complete |

B. Draw a line to match the word and its definition.

1. away from others   a. divide
2. to join together   b. pajamas
3. opposed to   c. degree
4. a vegetable that grows underground   d. against
5. to fix a mistake   e. combine
6. clothes worn while sleeping   f. alone
7. a unit for measuring the temperature   g. potato
8. to separate into parts   h. correct

C. Write a definition for the word *debate*.

_____

_____

Review It!
unstressed syllables
initial schwa

Name _____

Fill in the circle by the word that best completes each sentence.

A City Parade

1. Our city's Fourth of July _____ is a big event.

    Ⓐ perform   Ⓑ potato   Ⓒ parade

2. A few _____ officers on motorcycles led the parade.

    Ⓐ positions   Ⓑ police   Ⓒ polites

3. They ride _____ of the mayor, who waves from a red, white, and blue car.

    Ⓐ ahead   Ⓑ along   Ⓒ alone

4. High school bands _____ lively music that makes people clap.

    Ⓐ parade   Ⓑ perform   Ⓒ persist

5. Local scouts march and hold banners that _____ one troop from another.

    Ⓐ supply   Ⓑ division   Ⓒ divide

6. The sounds of drums and horns _____ with cheering and shouting.

    Ⓐ complete   Ⓑ compare   Ⓒ combine

7. Riders ride on horses that do not seem _____ of the crowds and noise.

    Ⓐ against   Ⓑ afraid   Ⓒ along

8. The parade ends with a big Statue of Liberty posed _____ an American flag.

    Ⓐ against   Ⓑ address   Ⓒ alert

Learn It!
unstressed syllables

Name _____

Final Schwa + /n/ and Schwa + /l/

The schwa sound is often heard in an unstressed syllable at the end of a word. The final schwa + /n/ sound can be spelled **en**, **in**, or **on**.
Listen for the schwa + /n/ sounds in these words:

dozen	robin	season
doz | ən	rob | ən	sea | sən

The final schwa + /l/ sound can be spelled **le**, **al**, **el**, or **il**.
Listen for the schwa + /l/ sounds in these words:

angle	global	label	pencil
an | gəl	glo | bəl	la | bəl	pen | səl

A. Read each word out loud. Circle the letters that spell the schwa + /n/ sound or the schwa + /l/ sound.

margin	cable	human	local
simple	title	raisin	gerbil
bacon	lemon	nickel	happen

B. Use words from above to fill in the chart.

Schwa + /n/ sound	Schwa + /l/ sound

Syllable Patterns
Phonics

Practice It!
unstressed syllables
final schwa + /n/ or /l/

What Is It?

A. Read each word out loud. Circle the letters that spell the schwa + /n/ sound or the schwa + /l/ sound.

person	castle	candle	cousin	middle
dozen	slogan	lemon	final	cable

B. Read the clue. Choose a word above to fill in the lines. Then read the words out loud.

1. This home has towers.   __ __ __ __ __ __

2. This is the usual number of eggs in a carton.   __ __ __ __ __

3. This is the part that is the center.   __ __ __ __ __ __

4. This is usually made of wax.   __ __ __ __ __ __

5. Your aunt's child is your ____.   __ __ __ __ __ __

6. This wire carries power to TVs.   __ __ __ __ __

7. This fruit goes with iced tea.   __ __ __ __ __

8. This is a human being.   __ __ __ __ __ __

C. Write a clue for the word *parade*.

_____

_____

Review It!

unstressed syllables
final schwa + /n/ or /l/

Name _____

Fill in the circle by the word that best completes each sentence.

Getting into Trouble

1. Who would have thought a pencil could get me into _____?

    Ⓐ trouble Ⓑ bubble Ⓒ double

2. I took a _____ from my brother Jorge's desk to do my homework.

    Ⓐ margin Ⓑ final Ⓒ pencil

3. Jorge takes the _____ bus home from his job after school.

    Ⓐ civil Ⓑ local Ⓒ easel

4. Today, he walked in the door at 5 o'clock and went upstairs as _____.

    Ⓐ casual Ⓑ usual Ⓒ simple

5. "Who took my pencil?" he shouted at _____ his normal sound.

    Ⓐ happen Ⓑ trouble Ⓒ double

6. "What's so _____ about that pencil?" I shouted back. "Just use another one."

    Ⓐ stencil Ⓑ special Ⓒ normal

7. "Rosa gave me that pencil the first time we sat together at the lunch _____," Jorge said.

    Ⓐ table Ⓑ easel Ⓒ label

8. I gave Jorge the pencil right away, because using it could have been my _____ act!

    Ⓐ usual Ⓑ casual Ⓒ final

Syllable Patterns
Phonics

Learn It!
unstressed syllables

Name _____

Final Schwa + /r/

The schwa sound is often heard in an unstressed syllable at the end of a word. The final schwa + /r/ sound can be spelled **ar**, **er**, or **or**. The final schwa + /r/ sounds like /ur/.

| lunar | shower | favor |
| lu \| nər | show \| ər | fa \| vər |

A. Read each word out loud. Circle the letters that spell the schwa + /r/ sound.

sugar	differ	motor	chapter
temper	harbor	collar	mayor
feather	solar	bother	cellar

B. Fill in the missing unstressed syllables to form the words above.

so_____   tem_____   col_____

may_____   sug_____   har_____

mo_____   dif_____   chap_____

cel_____   both_____   feath_____

Syllable Patterns
Phonics

Practice It!

unstressed syllables
final schwa + /r/

Name _____

Crossword Time!

A. Read each word. Circle the letters that spell the schwa + /r/ sound in the final syllable.

> doctor   tender   ladder   flavor   lunar
> mayor   lobster   solar   temper   chapter

B. Use words above to complete the crossword puzzle.

Across

1. having to do with the moon
2. a person trained to help the sick
6. a large shellfish used as food
7. a person who runs a city

Down

1. an object used to climb up and down
3. a part of a book
4. what gives food its taste
5. having to do with the sun

Review It!

unstressed syllables
final schwa + /r/

Name _____

Fill in the circle by the word that best completes each sentence.

A Clean Harbor

1. When she ran for office, our _____ promised to help our city.

    Ⓐ manner Ⓑ mayor Ⓒ manor

2. She had plans to get rid of all the pollution in our _____.

    Ⓐ hammer Ⓑ harbor Ⓒ hanger

3. The mayor became the _____ of "Help Our Harbor" day.

    Ⓐ creator Ⓑ collar Ⓒ crusher

4. On that day, an _____ spoke to the crowds that gathered at the harbor.

    Ⓐ burglar Ⓑ motor Ⓒ actor

5. He made an _____ to help pay for the changes that were needed.

    Ⓐ outer Ⓑ offer Ⓒ other

6. The litter, which is a _____ problem, would be removed.

    Ⓐ mover Ⓑ molar Ⓒ major

7. _____ would be used to make a covered picnic area.

    Ⓐ Lumber Ⓑ Temper Ⓒ Summer

8. One day our harbor will be a place to enjoy in any kind of _____.

    Ⓐ wonder Ⓑ whisker Ⓒ weather

Read It!
unstressed syllables

Lauren's Horrible Day

Lauren's day began with a thump. She had been fast asleep. All of a sudden, something pushed against the middle of her back. Lauren tumbled onto the floor. Her dog Mabel had taken over the bed.

Lauren looked at the clock and screeched. She had forgotten to set the alarm! Now she rushed to finish her school project.

Lauren placed her model of a coral reef on the floor and worked fast. She set the clams and mussels in place. Then she squirted some glitter glue to make a label. A cold wet nose pushed Lauren's arm. Glitter glue flew across the reef.

"Mabel! Look what you made me do!" yelled Lauren. She grabbed a wrinkled tissue to wipe up the mess. Pieces of tissue stuck to the glue. The coral reef looked as if a volcano had covered it in ashes. Lauren groaned. Mabel whined.

"I better let you outside. All I need is another mess!" said Lauren. She let Mabel into the yard. Then Lauren hurried to the kitchen table and stuffed down some cereal.

Getting to the bus stop took several minutes longer than usual. Carrying the reef wasn't easy. A small chunk broke off as Lauren got to her seat.

The rest of the day was terrible, too. At lunch her pizza fell on her shirt. She put sugar on her fries instead of salt. Worst of all, Lauren had done the wrong chapter of math for homework.

When Lauren got home, she saw that her gerbil had escaped from its cage. Two hours later, Mom screamed. She found the gerbil curled up asleep in a soup ladle.

Lauren was happy to go to bed that night. At last her horrible day was over. Mabel stretched out beside her. Then Lauren felt something pushing against the middle of her back.

Syllable Patterns
Phonics

Apply It!
unstressed syllables

Name _____

Now Try This...

1. Look back at the story. Write four words that end in each sound.

Schwa + /l/ sound	Schwa + /n/ sound

2. Why did Lauren tumble out of bed?

   _____

   _____

3. Do you think Lauren's horrible day has ended? Explain your answer.

   _____

   _____

4. Tell two things that Lauren could have prevented from happening.

   a. Lauren could have prevented _____

      if she had _____.

   b. Lauren could have prevented _____

      if she had _____.

5. Practice reading two long paragraphs in the story. Then read them to your teacher.

Syllable Patterns
Phonics

Recognizing Word Parts and Their Meanings

Plurals and Inflectional Endings 219

Possessives and Contractions 235

Affixes and Compound Words 245

High-Frequency Words 267

Plurals and Inflectional Endings

Overview
The **Plurals and Inflectional Endings** section has two purposes: 1) to help students recognize plural forms of nouns and their meanings; and 2) to help students recognize regular verb endings that indicate the past and present tenses and irregular verb forms.

Teaching Tips
You may want to use the following techniques to introduce the concepts in this section:

Plural Forms *pages 221–226*
Review with students the concept of singular and plural nouns. Ask students to complete the following sentence frames with things they see in the room: *I see one (book). Now I see two (books).* Write students' responses on the board, in two columns labeled Singular and Plural. Give prompts so that students elicit a few words whose spelling changes from *f* to *v* in their plural form (*leaf, leaves*) and a few nouns that change completely in their plural form (*child, children*).

Inflectional Endings: *–ed* and *–ing* *pages 227–229*
Make two columns on the board, and title one column Present Action and the other Past Action. On another area of the board, write three cities and say, "I am listing three cities." After you finish writing, say, "I listed three cities." Write the words *listing* and *listed* in the appropriate column. Repeat the process with students, acting out other verbs. While verbs are listed, call students' attention to a word that changes its spelling before the ending is added. For example: If a verb ends in a short vowel and a consonant, note that the consonant is doubled before adding *–ed* or *–ing* (*dropped, dropping*).

Irregular Verb Forms *pages 230–234*
Write a pair of sentence frames on the board and model the completion. For example:

> Right now, I see a computer. Yesterday, I (saw) a computer.

Repeat the process with sentence frames for *have, do, know,* and other irregular verbs used in everyday speaking. Have students take turns completing the sentence frames as you write the past and present forms on the board under the column heads Present and Past.

Rule Breakers
Looking for regular plural and inflectional endings can help students break words into readable chunks. Irregular verbs and nouns with irregular plural endings, however, are rule breakers that students need to memorize. Keep a list of those nouns and verbs in the room where they can be read frequently. Invite students to add other irregular words to the list as they encounter them.

Pretest
noun and verb endings

Name _____

A. Fill in the circle next to the **plural noun** that correctly completes each sentence.

1. Leo likes learning about the _____.
   - Ⓐ planet
   - Ⓑ planets
   - Ⓒ planetes

2. No two giraffes have the same kind of _____.
   - Ⓐ patchs
   - Ⓑ patchez
   - Ⓒ patches

3. The dentist showed me how best to clean my _____.
   - Ⓐ tooths
   - Ⓑ teeth
   - Ⓒ teethes

4. The earthquake knocked books off their _____.
   - Ⓐ shelves
   - Ⓑ shelfs
   - Ⓒ shelfes

5. My teacher had worked in three African _____.
   - Ⓐ countryes
   - Ⓑ countrys
   - Ⓒ countries

B. Fill in the circle next to the correct **verb** that completes each sentence.

1. Chad _____ the question correctly and won the prize.
   - Ⓐ answerred
   - Ⓑ answered
   - Ⓒ answeried

2. I'm feeling better because Ms. Ramirez _____ by to see me.
   - Ⓐ stopped
   - Ⓑ stoped
   - Ⓒ stopping

3. Lacey _____ to beat the throw to second base.
   - Ⓐ hurryed
   - Ⓑ huried
   - Ⓒ hurried

4. The first baseman _____ the ball into the dirt, and Lacey was safe.
   - Ⓐ thrown
   - Ⓑ throwed
   - Ⓒ threw

5. Gavin was _____ his sister to trade chores with him.
   - Ⓐ begged
   - Ⓑ begging
   - Ⓒ begs

Plurals and Inflectional Endings
Word Study

Learn It!
plural nouns

Name _____

Plural Noun Endings: –s, –es

A noun in its singular form shows one.
A noun in its plural form shows more than one.

To make most nouns plural, you add **s** to the end of the word.

Singular	Plural
planet	planet**s**

Some nouns need spelling changes to form the plural.

- If a word ends in **x, s, z, ch,** or **sh,** you usually add **es**.

    mat<u>ch</u> ⟶ match**es**

    circu<u>s</u> ⟶ circus**es**

- If a word ends in a **vowel** and **y**, you add **s**.

    mon<u>key</u> ⟶ monkey**s**

- If a word ends in a **consonant** and **y**, you change the **y** to **i** and add **es**.

    po<u>ny</u> ⟶ pon**ies**

A. Read each word out loud. Listen to the sound of the plural ending. Circle the **s** or **es**.

planets	lobbies	foxes	valleys
countries	brushes	cities	glasses
watches	dreams	jackets	benches

B. Write the plural form of each word.

hour _____   candy _____   party _____

speech _____   tray _____   mix _____

box _____   dish _____   mask _____

Plurals and Inflectional Endings
Word Study

Practice It!
plural nouns
–s, –es

Name _____

Find Those Words!

A. Read each word out loud. Listen for the sound of the plural ending. Circle the **s** or **es**.

| puppies | monkeys | boxes | matches | brushes |
| parents | artists | pockets | houses | classes |

B. Circle the words above in the puzzle. The words can read down, across, or diagonally.

```
P A B C H O U S P A A
O R R L P O C K P R O
C T S I P A R E N T S
K I H S E S S S S I S
E S E S Y E E E O S I
T T S E S H H M S T S
S K K S S C O I M S O
S O A U T B O X E S O
M L R A P U P P I E S
C B M E M O N K E Y S
H O U S E S C L A S O
```

C. Write nine of the circled words on the lines.

_____ _____ _____

_____ _____ _____

_____ _____ _____

Plurals and Inflectional Endings
Word Study

Review It!
plural nouns
–s, –es

Name _____

Fill in the circle by the word that best completes each sentence.

Free Pets

1. My Uncle Walt raises _____ for pets.
   - Ⓐ rabbits
   - Ⓑ ants
   - Ⓒ rattles

2. He gives them away to _____ who promise to care for them.
   - Ⓐ faxes
   - Ⓑ families
   - Ⓒ cities

3. Everyone seems to want the cute little _____!
   - Ⓐ beaches
   - Ⓑ bunnies
   - Ⓒ buses

4. Children's _____ need to give permission before Uncle Walt gives them a bunny.
   - Ⓐ patches
   - Ⓑ parrots
   - Ⓒ parents

5. On Saturdays, Uncle Walt teaches _____ to people who own rabbits.
   - Ⓐ classes
   - Ⓑ clashes
   - Ⓒ glasses

6. He shows how to groom the pets and brush their _____.
   - Ⓐ capes
   - Ⓑ coaches
   - Ⓒ coats

7. People learn how to build _____ and see how to keep them clean.
   - Ⓐ hunches
   - Ⓑ hutches
   - Ⓒ hatches

8. After class, Uncle Walt _____ hutches that need repair.
   - Ⓐ boxes
   - Ⓑ mixes
   - Ⓒ fixes

Learn It!
other plural forms

Name _____

Other Plural Forms

Some nouns need spelling changes to form the plural.

- When a word ends in **f** or **fe**, you usually change the **f** to **v** and add **es**. You can hear the /v/ sound.

    li<u>fe</u> ⟶ li**ves**   cal<u>f</u> ⟶ cal**ves**

Some words change completely in the plural form.

   child ⟶ children   foot ⟶ feet

Some words do not change in the plural form.

   deer ⟶ deer   fish ⟶ fish

A. Read each plural noun out loud. Circle the plural nouns made by changing the *f* to *v* and adding **es**.

fish	moose	shrimp	leaves
teeth	geese	loaves	wolves
women	shelves	sheep	mice

B. Write the plural form of each word.

Singular	Plural	Singular	Plural
moose		goose	
shelf		mouse	
tooth		shrimp	
loaf		fish	
sheep		wolf	
woman		leaf	

Plurals and Inflectional Endings
Word Study

Practice It!
other plural forms

Name _____

Make Those Matches!

A. Read each plural noun out loud. Circle the ones that change completely in the plural form.

| wives | bacon | children | leaves | shrimp |
| women | knives | wheat | feet | scarves |

B. Read each clue. Draw a line to the word that goes with the clue.

1. They wrap around necks.   a. knives
2. These tree parts make food for the tree.   b. feet
3. It is grown to make into bread.   c. leaves
4. You stand on these.   d. women
5. This has a shell, claws, and a tail, but it is not a turtle.   e. children
6. These are used to chop food.   f. wives
7. These women have said, "I do."   g. wheat
8. This sizzles when it cooks.   h. bacon
9. This is what adults used to be.   i. shrimp
10. This is what girls grow up to be.   j. scarves

C. Write a clue for the word *mice*.

_____

_____

Review It!
other plural forms

Name _____

Fill in the circle by the word that best completes each sentence.

Loaves for Lives

1. Many men, women, and _____ in our city go to sleep cold and hungry every night.

    Ⓐ child   Ⓑ children   Ⓒ childs

2. The Food Bank tries to save _____ by collecting food and clothing for the homeless.

    Ⓐ lines   Ⓑ lives   Ⓒ livers

3. Boxes and cans of food are stacked on _____ and are used to fill food baskets.

    Ⓐ shells   Ⓑ shelves   Ⓒ shelters

4. Many bakeries give bread that is made into _____.

    Ⓐ sandals   Ⓑ sandboxes   Ⓒ sandwiches

5. Men and _____ serve soup and sandwiches to people who come to the Food Bank.

    Ⓐ women   Ⓑ woman   Ⓒ wolves

6. Other people knit _____ and sweaters for homeless children.

    Ⓐ scars   Ⓑ leaves   Ⓒ scarves

7. The Food Bank tries to get the local _____ to visit.

    Ⓐ mazes   Ⓑ media   Ⓒ medals

8. The media's news inspires _____ to help the homeless.

    Ⓐ person   Ⓑ people   Ⓒ peoples

Learn It!
verb endings

Name _____

Verb Endings: –ed, –ing

A verb ending can show when an action takes place.

Present Action **Past Action**
jump**ing** jump**ed**

Some verbs need spelling changes before adding *ing* or *ed*.

- If the verb ends in a **consonant** and **e**, drop the **e** and add *ing* or *ed*.
  taste ⟶ tasting   taste ⟶ tasted
- If the verb ends in a **short vowel** and a **consonant**, double the final consonant and add *ing* or *ed*.
  drop ⟶ dropping   drop ⟶ dropped
- If a verb ends in a **consonant** and **y**, keep the **y** before adding *ing*.
  hurry ⟶ hurrying
  Change the **y** to **i** before adding *ed*.
  hurry ⟶ hurried

A. Read each word out loud. Circle the verbs that show an action that happened in the past.

spied   worried   tried   burying

wrapped   shopped   adding   traded

shopping   danced   changing   wanted

B. Rewrite each verb with the endings below.

	Past Action: Add –ed	Present Action: Add –ing
cry		
melt		
brag		
deny		
taste		
nod		

Plurals and Inflectional Endings
Word Study

Practice It!
verb endings
–ed, –ing

Name _____

Crossword Time!

A. Read each verb out loud. Circle the ones that show an action going on now, in the present.

adding	danced	shopping	melted	tried
spied	bragged	wanted	denying	trading

B. Use words above to complete the crossword puzzle.

Down

1. boasted
2. combining one thing with another
4. exchanging one thing for another
6. snooped

Across

3. wished for; desired
5. moved in time to music
7. buying things
8. made an effort

Plurals and Inflectional Endings
Word Study

Review It!

verb endings
–ed, –ing

Name _____

Fill in the circle by the word that best completes each sentence.

Have You Tried Dancing?

1. Leo watched a dance contest, and he _____ to learn how to dance.
   - Ⓐ wanting
   - Ⓑ want
   - Ⓒ wanted

2. Leo found out that Mrs. Rayner was _____ dance at the youth club.
   - Ⓐ teaching
   - Ⓑ teaming
   - Ⓒ teasing

3. He heard that she was _____ classes for kids 10 to 13 years old.
   - Ⓐ closing
   - Ⓑ offering
   - Ⓒ ordering

4. Leo's mother took him to the youth club, and he _____ up for dance classes.
   - Ⓐ sighed
   - Ⓑ signed
   - Ⓒ signing

5. The first class was hard, as Leo _____ to keep up with the other kids.
   - Ⓐ tried
   - Ⓑ tied
   - Ⓒ trimmed

6. The more Leo _____ the steps, the better he got.
   - Ⓐ practicing
   - Ⓑ practice
   - Ⓒ practiced

7. After Mrs. Rayner _____ up the last class, she asked Leo to stay.
   - Ⓐ wrapped
   - Ⓑ worked
   - Ⓒ wrapping

8. "You are a good dancer," Mrs. Rayner said. Then she _____ Leo to join a harder class.
   - Ⓐ inviting
   - Ⓑ inspected
   - Ⓒ invited

Learn It!
irregular verbs

Name _____

Other Verb Forms That Show the Past

Some verbs do not have an **–ed** ending to show that an action happened in the past. These verbs are called irregular verbs.
Irregular verbs change completely in their past form.

Present Form	Past Form
make	made
know	knew
do	did

Each irregular verb below is in the past form. Read each word out loud. Then write it in the chart.

| thought | went | broke | caught | slept |
| were | was | threw | sang | had |

Present Form	Past Form
throw	
think	
sleep	
go	
have	
sing	
is	
are	
break	
catch	

Plurals and Inflectional Endings
Word Study

Practice It!
irregular verbs

Name _____

Who Knew?

A. Draw a line to match the verbs.

Present Form	Past Form
1. blow	a. sang
2. say	b. rode
3. teach	c. taught
4. ride	d. bought
5. bring	e. blew
6. buy	f. was
7. is	g. said
8. sing	h. brought

B. Write a paragraph about teaching someone to sing. Write it in the past tense, and use at least three of the verbs above.

_____

_____

_____

_____

_____

Review It!
irregular verbs

Name _____

Fill in the circle by the word that best completes each sentence.

You Threw *What* Away?

1. I cannot believe what my mom _____ yesterday.
   - Ⓐ do
   - Ⓑ did
   - Ⓒ done

2. She cleaned my room, which was nice, but she _____ away some of my stuff!
   - Ⓐ throw
   - Ⓑ throws
   - Ⓒ threw

3. Mom _____ that she threw away only the junk.
   - Ⓐ saying
   - Ⓑ said
   - Ⓒ say

4. She _____ a pile of rocks under my bed and got rid of it!
   - Ⓐ found
   - Ⓑ flew
   - Ⓒ formed

5. "But that _____ my rock collection," I complained.
   - Ⓐ were
   - Ⓑ went
   - Ⓒ was

6. "You _____ I was collecting rocks," I whined.
   - Ⓐ known
   - Ⓑ knew
   - Ⓒ knows

7. "I _____ your collection was in a box, where it is supposed to be," Mom replied.
   - Ⓐ thought
   - Ⓑ though
   - Ⓒ through

8. "Don't tell me that pile of dirt was something you _____ saving, too!" Mom said.
   - Ⓐ is
   - Ⓑ was
   - Ⓒ were

Plurals and Inflectional Endings
Word Study

Read It!
noun and verb endings

The Shopping Trip

The date was circled in red on the calendar. Tomorrow was Mom and Dad's wedding anniversary. Sam and Maya wanted to buy a gift for their parents. They begged their sister Lea to take them shopping at the mall. Lea agreed but said they had to be home in a couple of hours.

The three kids started in a bookstore. Sam headed to the mystery books. He knew that Dad loved mysteries. Mom loved art, so Maya looked at books about artists. A lot of choices filled the shelves, but the three agreed. Nothing seemed right for *both* Mom and Dad.

Next, they stopped in a kitchen store. They looked at glasses, dishes, and a set of knives. The knives would be great for Mom, who liked cooking. But Dad never made any meals.

Sam spotted a clothing store. "Check out the window. We can buy them matching shirts!" he shouted.

"We don't know their sizes," Maya pointed out.

Maya spied a candy store. Sam said candy was a bad idea because Dad was trying to diet. Lea sighed.

She led Sam and Maya into a camera shop. "Mom and Dad's camera broke. Buying them a camera would be great," said Lea.

The three combined their money. They didn't have enough to buy a camera. Turning to leave the shop, Maya saw some picture frames. "I have an idea," she said. She was carrying a box wrapped in pretty paper when they left the store.

The next day, Mom and Dad unwrapped their gift. They loved the framed photo of their three smiling children.

Apply It!
noun and verb endings

Name _____

Now Try This...

1. Write each story word in the column that describes its ending.

> children   shelves   stopped   begged   saw
> sizes   broke   mysteries   spied   said

Plural Nouns	Irregular Verbs–Past Form	Regular Verbs–Past Form

2. What is one reason why Sam, Maya, and Lea were having problems buying a gift?

_____

_____

3. Why might parents love a framed photo of their children as a gift?

_____

_____

4. Based on what you read, write a conclusion you can draw about Sam and Maya.

Sam and Maya are _____.

Write a fact from the story that supports your conclusion.

They _____

_____.

5. Practice reading two long paragraphs in the story. Then read them to your teacher.

Plurals and Inflectional Endings
Word Study

Possessives and Contractions

Overview
The purpose of the **Possessives and Contractions** section is to help students decode and comprehend words that contain an apostrophe.

Teaching Tips
You may want to use the following techniques to introduce the concepts in this section:

Possessives *pages 237–239*
Review the concept of ownership by pointing to items in the room and identifying them by their owners (e.g., *Mia's desk; Julio's folder; the girls' photo*). Call attention to the /s/ sound heard at the end of each "owner" (*Mia's, Julio's, girls'*). Have volunteers give additional examples of classroom ownership, and write those on the board. Explain that the /s/ sound and an apostrophe signal ownership, or possession.

Contractions *pages 240–244*
- Read the following sentences to students, and then ask them to restate the sentences using contractions:

    I cannot go with you.
    Are you not going to the mall?
    There is my dog.
    I have not seen that movie.
    I am wearing my new jeans.

- Write "they are" on the board, and model erasing the *a* and replacing it with an apostrophe. Say the new word. Then have students work with a partner to do the same steps with these word pairs:

    we are; what is; she will; is not; I have; you would

  After checking students' work, ask them to look at the contractions they wrote and to answer these questions: *How many words get combined to form a contraction?* (two) *Is there a rule about the number of letters that get replaced with an apostrophe?* (no) *Do you hear the letter sounds that are replaced by the apostrophe?* (no)

Rule Breakers
Can't is a common contraction that is the contracted form of one word—*cannot*. Explain to students that word forms can change over time. *Can* and *not* originally were spelled as two words, but at some point *can* and *not* became the single word *cannot*.

Pretest
singular and plural possessives; contractions

Name _____

A. Fill in the circle next to the word that correctly spells the possessive form of the missing noun.

1. My _____ car is in the shop.
   - Ⓐ mom's
   - Ⓑ moms
   - Ⓒ moms'

2. The _____ museum is nearby.
   - Ⓐ childrens
   - Ⓑ children's
   - Ⓒ childrens'

3. _____ cat plays with yarn.
   - Ⓐ Pedro's
   - Ⓑ Pedros'
   - Ⓒ Pedros

4. My two _____ beds were unmade.
   - Ⓐ brother's
   - Ⓑ brothers
   - Ⓒ brothers'

5. All the _____ uniforms were clean.
   - Ⓐ players'
   - Ⓑ players
   - Ⓒ player's

6. We stored _____ computer for the summer.
   - Ⓐ everyones
   - Ⓑ everyones'
   - Ⓒ everyone's

B. Fill in the circle next to the contraction for each pair of words.

1. they are   Ⓐ they're   Ⓑ they's   Ⓒ they've

2. you have   Ⓐ you'ave   Ⓑ you're   Ⓒ you've

3. we will   Ⓐ wel'l   Ⓑ we'll   Ⓒ we've

4. he has   Ⓐ he's   Ⓑ he'd   Ⓒ he'll

5. she would   Ⓐ she'll   Ⓑ she'ld   Ⓒ she'd

Possessives and Contractions
Word Study

Learn It!
possessives

Name _____

Nouns That Show Ownership

A possessive form of a noun shows that the noun owns something. Possessive nouns have an **'** (apostrophe).

Here are rules for making a noun show possession:

- When the noun is singular, add **'s** to form the possessive.

Singular Noun	Singular Possessive	Example
spider	spider**'s**	spider**'s** web

- When the noun is plural but does <u>not</u> end in s, add **'s**.

Plural Noun	Plural Possessive	Example
geese	geese**'s**	geese**'s** wings

- When the noun is plural and does end in s, add just the **'**.

Plural Noun	Plural Possessive	Example
hippos	hippo**s'**	hippo**s'** ears

A. Read each word out loud. Circle the singular possessive nouns. Underline the plural possessive nouns.

spider's	brothers'	women's	bird's
children's	door's	countries'	coaches'
shoes'	Marie's	sailors'	city's

B. Read each noun. Write the ending that shows the noun's possessive form.

spider____	spiders____	child____	children____
girl____	girls____	birds____	men____
flower____	cats____	artist____	artists____

Possessives and Contractions
Word Study

Practice It!
possessives
singular and plural

Name _____

Which Possessive Is It?

A. Circle the singular possessive nouns. Underline the plural possessive nouns.

bat's	teacher's	sister's	store's	twin's
bats'	teachers'	sisters'	stores'	twins'

B. Write a word from above that best completes each sentence.

1. The _____ desk is in the corner of the classroom.

2. The _____ parking lot is behind the school.

3. The sound of hundreds of _____ wings is scary.

4. A _____ wings are made of thick skin.

5. My two _____ bedrooms are upstairs.

6. My _____ car is black, and my brother's car is blue.

7. All of the _____ signs in the mall are neon.

8. The _____ lights were on, so I thought it was open.

9. One of the _____ teeth is missing.

10. Both of the _____ shirts are too small to wear.

Possessives and Contractions
Word Study

Review It!

possessives
singular and plural

Name _____

Fill in the circle by the word that best completes each sentence.

Kelly's Poems

1. _____ sister Kelly likes to write poems.
   - Ⓐ Davids'
   - Ⓑ David's
   - Ⓒ Davids

2. Some of _____ poems are funny and some are serious.
   - Ⓐ Kelly's
   - Ⓑ Kellys'
   - Ⓒ Kellys

3. Ms. Chan, Kelly's teacher, wanted Kelly to enter her _____ poetry-writing contest.
   - Ⓐ cities'
   - Ⓑ city's
   - Ⓒ cities

4. Kelly got her _____ permission to enter the contest.
   - Ⓐ parents
   - Ⓑ parent's
   - Ⓒ parents'

5. She told Ms. Chan about being inspired by her _____ poetry.
   - Ⓐ grandmothers
   - Ⓑ grandmother's
   - Ⓒ grandmother

6. Ms. Chan suggested that Kelly write a poem about her grandmother and send it to the _____ judges.
   - Ⓐ contests'
   - Ⓑ contest
   - Ⓒ contest's

7. Kelly's poem won a blue ribbon in the _____ group.
   - Ⓐ children's
   - Ⓑ childrens'
   - Ⓒ childrens

8. Her _____ pride in Kelly was great!
   - Ⓐ family
   - Ⓑ family's
   - Ⓒ familys'

Learn It!
contractions

Name _____

Contractions

A contraction is a word formed from two words by leaving out one or more letters. An ' (apostrophe) takes the place of the missing letters. Read these common contractions:

you are	**you're**
here is	**here's**
you have	**you've**
Joe will	**Joe'll**
could not	**couldn't**
I would	**I'd**
I had	**I'd**

A. Read each contraction. Then write the two words that form the contraction.

1. they'll _____
2. we're _____
3. it's _____
4. haven't _____
5. I've _____

6. you'd _____
7. don't _____
8. Manny'll _____
9. isn't _____
10. who's _____

B. Write the contraction for each pair of words.

1. I am _____
2. they are _____
3. you have _____
4. should not _____

5. she is _____
6. he has _____
7. they will _____
8. are not _____

Practice It!
contractions

Name _____

It's Contraction Time

A. Match the words and their contractions.

1. they had
2. would not
3. she would
4. it will
5. he has
6. we have
7. you are
8. that is

a. it'll
b. you're
c. they'd
d. we've
e. that's
f. she'd
g. wouldn't
h. he's

B. Read the paragraph. Cross out each pair of words in parentheses, and then write the contraction on the line above them.

Have you watched people skateboarding? _____ a real sport that
                                          (It is)

many kids practice for hours. _____ a place in our town's park _____
                               (There is)   (that is)

set aside for skateboarders. _____ been there many times with my mom.
                              (I have)

_____ a big skateboarding fan. She _____ given me permission to
(She is)   (has not)

skateboard at the park. "Next year, _____ be able to skateboard here if
                                     (you will)

you practice enough and get really good," Mom promised. I think _____
                                                                  (I have)

gotten to be a very good skateboarder already, but _____ play it safe.
                                                    (I will)

Review It!
contractions

Name _____

Fill in the circle by the word that best completes each sentence.

You Shouldn't Have

1. I _____ know what to get Gramps for his birthday.
   - Ⓐ shouldn't
   - Ⓑ didn't
   - Ⓒ haven't

2. _____ always wanted to do something special for him.
   - Ⓐ I've
   - Ⓑ I'll
   - Ⓒ I'm

3. "_____ the perfect gift?" I wondered.
   - Ⓐ Whats'
   - Ⓑ What's
   - Ⓒ Whats

4. I knew that Gramps loves dogs. _____ always reading dog magazines.
   - Ⓐ He'd
   - Ⓑ He's
   - Ⓒ He'll

5. _____ spend hours reading about the Boxer, which is the breed he likes best.
   - Ⓐ He'll
   - Ⓑ He's
   - Ⓒ He've

6. On the day of Gramps' birthday, I _____ wait to give him his gift.
   - Ⓐ don't
   - Ⓑ haven't
   - Ⓒ couldn't

7. "_____ your present, Gramps," I said, as a Boxer puppy ran to greet him.
   - Ⓐ Here'd
   - Ⓑ Here's
   - Ⓒ Here'll

8. "Come on, boy. _____ have some fun!" said Gramps to his new pet.
   - Ⓐ They're
   - Ⓑ Let'll
   - Ⓒ Let's

Read It!

singular and plural possessives; contractions

What'll He Do Next?

Rosa loved walking in the woods with her friend Carla. Today, they hadn't planned on having Rosa's little brother tag along. Pedro was such a pest! He wouldn't stay with them. He kept stopping to look at spiders' webs. And he'd dash off the path to chase a bug.

Sure enough, Rosa noticed that Pedro wasn't with them. "Pedro!" she began to yell.

Pedro answered. "You've got to see this! I've found an underground cave!"

The girls followed the sound of his voice. They ran to reach him.

"I can't see much because it's too dark. But I think there's a path," said Pedro.

"You shouldn't be down there! Come up right now," said Rosa.

"Okay. Don't get excited," said Pedro. He tried to get out, but he couldn't reach the opening. Rosa hung over the edge of the cave, but Pedro couldn't grab her hands.

"I'll come down and give you a boost," said Rosa. "You stay up here, Carla, and help pull us up."

Rosa dropped into the cave. "Can't we explore?" begged Pedro. "We'll go just a short way."

Rosa was about to answer when a rock tumbled from the cave's roof. "We've got to get out of here!" she yelled.

Rosa grabbed Pedro's waist. She pushed him toward Carla's waiting arms. Dirt and stones hit Rosa's head as she tried to climb up.

Carla and Pedro pulled Rosa out of the cave. Pedro cried when he saw his sister's cut face. "It's my fault you're hurt! I won't go off on my own next time. I promise."

Possessives and Contractions
Word Study

Apply It!
singular and plural possessives;
contractions

Name _____

Now Try This...

1. Look back at the story. Find five contractions and five possessives. List them in the chart.

Contractions	Possessives

2. What do you think Rosa was going to answer when Pedro begged to explore the cave? Tell why you think so.

   _____

   _____

3. Do you think Pedro will keep his promise not to go off on his own? _____

   Why do you think so? _____

   _____

4. How would you judge Pedro's actions during the walk?

   _____

   _____

5. Practice reading two long paragraphs in the story. Then read them to your teacher.

Possessives and Contractions
Word Study

Affixes and Compound Words

Overview
The **Affixes and Compound Words** section has two purposes: 1) to help students decode words by reading their familiar parts; and 2) to help students learn the meanings of common prefixes and suffixes as a strategy to determine the meaning of unfamiliar words. This section covers affixes added to base words, not to roots.

Teaching Tips
You may want to use the following techniques to introduce the concepts in this section:

Prefixes *pages 247–254*
Explain to students that prefixes are word parts added at the beginnings of words to form new words. Write the following base words on the board:

honest, stop, due, correct, fill, friendly

Then write the following prefixes on sticky-backed notes:

re, un, in, dis, non, over

Model for students how to make new words by adding the prefixes to the base words. Then for each new word, guide students in reading the prefix, the base word, and the two parts together.

Suffixes *pages 256–261*
Explain to students that suffixes are word parts added to the ends of words to make new words. Write the following base words on the board:

help, enjoy, fair, weak, cold, strange

Write the following suffixes on sticky-backed notes:

ly, er, est, less, ness, able

Place each suffix at the end of each base word. Have students say if it forms a new word. If it does, write the suffix after the base word. Then guide students in reading the new words by saying the suffix, the base word, and the two parts together.

Compound Words *pages 262–266*
Explain to students that some words are made up of two smaller words. List the following examples:

watchdog, carpool, afternoon, scrapbook

Model how to decode such words by reading the first smaller word, the second smaller word, and then the two words together.

Rule Breakers
Some words begin with the same letters as common prefixes, such as *uncle* and *rent,* but the letters do not form prefixes. Show students how to cover those letters to see if a real word is left over. If it is, the letters spell a prefix.

Pretest
prefixes

Name _____

Circle the prefix in the word. Then fill in the circle next to the correct meaning of the word.

1. reapply	Ⓐ not apply	Ⓑ apply once	Ⓒ apply again
2. preplan	Ⓐ plan ahead	Ⓑ plan again	Ⓒ not planned
3. unsafe	Ⓐ very safe	Ⓑ most safe	Ⓒ not safe
4. misread	Ⓐ read wrongly	Ⓑ read again	Ⓒ read too much
5. nonstop	Ⓐ does not stop	Ⓑ stops a lot	Ⓒ stops
6. incorrect	Ⓐ correct again	Ⓑ not correct	Ⓒ most correct
7. disobey	Ⓐ obey again	Ⓑ obey	Ⓒ not obey
8. imperfect	Ⓐ too perfect	Ⓑ not perfect	Ⓒ overly perfect
9. overpay	Ⓐ pay too much	Ⓑ pay again	Ⓒ not pay
10. unglued	Ⓐ over glued	Ⓑ glued wrongly	Ⓒ not glued

Affixes and Compound Words
Word Study

Learn It!
prefixes

Name _____

Prefixes: *pre-, re-, im-, in-, un-*

A prefix is a word part added at the beginning of a word.

prefix	+	word	=	new word
re	+	use	=	reuse

A prefix changes the meaning of the word.
Knowing the meaning of a prefix can help you figure out the word's meaning.

pre means "before"   **pre**game means "before the game"
re means "again"   **re**paint means "paint again"
im means "not"   **im**possible means "not possible"
in means "not"   **in**visible means "not visible"
un often means "not"   **un**friendly means "not friendly"

A. Read each word out loud. Circle the prefix. Share what you think each word means.

reapply	indirect	reset	unaware
unknown	precut	incorrect	reread
preplan	unhappy	prepay	improper

B. Write three words for each prefix. Use the words above. Then add your own words to the fourth row.

pre = before	*re* = again	*im* or *in* = not	*un* = not

Practice It!

prefixes
pre–, re–, im–, in–, un–

Name _____

Unscramble the Words!

A. Read each word out loud. Circle the prefixes. Share what you think each word means.

incomplete	prepay	previews	impolite
refill	imperfect	inactive	unable

B. Read the definition. Then unscramble the answer and write it on the lines.

1. not polite — poetilim — __ __ __ __ __ __ __
2. fill again — liferl — __ __ __ __ __ __
3. not active — vacintie — __ __ __ __ __ __ __ __
4. looks at ahead of time — swieverp — __ __ __ __ __ __ __ __
5. not able — alebnu — __ __ __ __ __ __
6. not complete — mocpleetni — __ __ __ __ __ __ __ __ __ __
7. pay for ahead of time — yapper — __ __ __ __ __ __
8. not right — recorctni — __ __ __ __ __ __ __ __ __

C. Unscramble the circled letters to answer the clue.

You do this to your seat belt before getting out of the car.

__ __ __ __ __ __ __ __

Affixes and Compound Words
Word Study

Review It!

prefixes
pre–, re–, im–, in–, un–

Name _____

Fill in the circle by the word that best completes each sentence.

Soccer Replay

1. Todd's soccer team _____ to Todd's house every year to watch the World Cup on TV.

    Ⓐ reviews   Ⓑ replays   Ⓒ returns

2. This year, everyone arrived early for a _____ party.

    Ⓐ disgame   Ⓑ pregame   Ⓒ regame

3. They recorded the game and _____ it later.

    Ⓐ replayed   Ⓑ restored   Ⓒ preplayed

4. It was _____ to hear the game because of the cheering.

    Ⓐ impolite   Ⓑ improper   Ⓒ impossible

5. The teams were really good, and the outcome often was _____.

    Ⓐ uncertain   Ⓑ unaware   Ⓒ unable

6. France's team played well, but Italy's players were _____ in skill.

    Ⓐ unhurt   Ⓑ unequal   Ⓒ unhappy

7. Todd's father was _____ about which team to root for.

    Ⓐ misdecided   Ⓑ undecided   Ⓒ imdecided

8. He was _____ to choose between the United States and Brazil.

    Ⓐ disable   Ⓑ misable   Ⓒ unable

Name _____

Prefixes: dis–, mis–, non–, over–

Every prefix has a meaning.
Knowing the meaning of a prefix can help you figure out the meaning of a word.

dis can mean "not" and "opposite of" **dis**honest means "not honest"
mis often means "wrongly" **mis**file means "file wrongly"
non means "not" **non**fiction means "not fiction"
over means "too much" **over**cook means "cook too much"

A. Read each word out loud. Circle the prefix. Share what you think each word means.

nonsmoking	disconnect	nonstop	overdo
overhear	dislike	misguide	nondrip
mistype	overthrow	misname	disappear

B. Write three words for each prefix. Use the words above. Then add your own words to the fourth row.

dis = not or opposite of	**mis** = wrongly	**non** = not	**over** = too much

Practice It!
prefixes
dis–, mis–, non–, over–

Name _____

Do Not Overlook the Clues!

A. Read each word out loud. Circle the prefix. Share what you think each word means.

| disappear | misread | nonsticky | overcharge | disobey |
| overdue | nonliving | misplace | dislike | nonstop |

B. Use words above to complete the crossword puzzle.

Across

1. goes on and on
4. to go out of sight
6. to put in the wrong place
7. late
8. to not like or care for

Down

2. a category for a rock
3. to charge too much
5. to read incorrectly

Review It!
prefixes
dis–, mis–, non–, over–

Name _____

Fill in the circle by the word that best completes each sentence.

Overbusy but Fun

1. A group of us worked _____ to put on our first play.

    Ⓐ nonstop Ⓑ nonslip Ⓒ nonsupport

2. At first everyone was scared and _____.

    Ⓐ dishonest Ⓑ discouraged Ⓒ discolored

3. The director helped us _____ our fears.

    Ⓐ overstep Ⓑ overcame Ⓒ overcome

4. He showed the actors how to be natural and how not to _____.

    Ⓐ overact Ⓑ overrate Ⓒ overlook

5. He worked with them so they didn't _____ their lines.

    Ⓐ misfile Ⓑ misread Ⓒ mistreat

6. The prop man learned not to _____ the props.

    Ⓐ misplace Ⓑ misorder Ⓒ mistreat

7. One actor practiced how to _____ through a trapdoor that went under the stage.

    Ⓐ disallow Ⓑ dislike Ⓒ disappear

8. Even though the work was _____, I loved doing it.

    Ⓐ nonpaying Ⓑ nonsticky Ⓒ nonliving

Affixes and Compound Words
Word Study

Read It!
prefixes

A Misadventure

Gil and Marc stood tall and listened carefully. They didn't want to disappoint Mrs. Silva. Their worries were unnecessary. She was pleased to hire the two pet sitters. Mrs. Silva was going away for a week. She needed them to feed her cat.

"I dislike leaving Sweetie at the vet's. She reacts badly to being locked in a cage," explained Mrs. Silva. Then she said, "How inconsiderate of me! You must be impatient to meet Sweetie. Follow me."

Mrs. Silva led the boys into her den. A large, unfriendly cat stared at them. As the boys got closer, Sweetie hissed. She definitely disliked them. Marc and Gil looked a little uncertain. Maybe the job was a mistake.

"I'll prepay you of course," said Mrs. Silva. "Sweetie is just unhappy that I'm going away." She reviewed what the boys needed to do. Then she added, "Sweetie always stays inside. *Never* let her out. It's too unsafe."

For six days, watching Sweetie was easy. She hissed at the boys, but she was inactive. On the last day, as the boys were ready to leave, Sweetie shot out the door. Marc and Gil misjudged her speed. They were unable to overtake her. Sweetie ran into some bushes and disappeared. The boys searched for her, but she never responded to their calls.

"Mrs. Silva is going to be very unhappy," said Marc.

"We'll have to return the money she gave us," added Gil.

Discouraged, the boys walked slowly back to Mrs. Silva's house. They wrote a note saying they were sorry for losing Sweetie. As they opened the door to leave, Sweetie strolled in. She seemed to have a smirk on her face.

Affixes and Compound Words
Word Study

Apply It!
prefixes

Name _____

Now Try This...

1. Look back at the story. Write three words for each prefix.

re–	
un–	
dis–	

2. What might be a reason why Mrs. Silva prepaid Gil and Marc?

   _____

   _____

3. Describe Marc and Gil. Use facts from the story to support your descriptions.

   Marc and Gil are _____ and _____.

   _____

   _____

   _____

4. Is it anyone's fault that Sweetie ran out the door? _____
   Explain your answer.

   _____

   _____

5. Practice reading two long paragraphs in the story. Then read them to your teacher.

Pretest
suffixes

Name _____

Circle the suffix in the word. Then fill in the circle next to the correct meaning of the word.

1. coldly	Ⓐ in a cold manner	Ⓑ without cold	Ⓒ more cold
2. jogger	Ⓐ able to jog	Ⓑ someone who jogs	Ⓒ a path for running
3. funniest	Ⓐ more funny	Ⓑ without fun	Ⓒ most funny
4. waterless	Ⓐ to be like water	Ⓑ someone who waters	Ⓒ without water
5. fixable	Ⓐ can't be fixed	Ⓑ can be fixed	Ⓒ someone who fixes things
6. weakness	Ⓐ the state of being weak	Ⓑ strong	Ⓒ not weak
7. rounder	Ⓐ most round	Ⓑ not round	Ⓒ more round
8. actor	Ⓐ someone who acts	Ⓑ without action	Ⓒ can be acted
9. thickest	Ⓐ not thick	Ⓑ more thick	Ⓒ most thick
10. warmer	Ⓐ most warm	Ⓑ more warm	Ⓒ not warm

Name _____

Learn It!
suffixes

Suffixes: –ly, –or, –er, –est

A suffix is a word part added at the end of a word.

word	+	suffix	=	new word
warm	+	er	=	warmer

A suffix changes the meaning of the word. Knowing the meaning of a suffix can help you figure out the meaning of a word.

ly means "in a certain manner"   sad**ly** means "in a sad manner"
or and **er** mean "someone who"   act**or** means "someone who acts"
er can mean "more"   loud**er** means "more loud"
est means "most"   loud**est** means "the most loud of all"

Adding a suffix sometimes changes the spelling of the word.

- If a word ends in silent **e**, drop the **e** before adding **er** or **est**.

    late ⟶ later   safe ⟶ safest

- If a word ends in a consonant + **y**, change the **y** to **i** before adding **er** or **est**.

    pretty ⟶ prettier   happy ⟶ happiest

A. Read each word out loud. Circle the suffix. Share what you think each word means.

visitor   thicker   slyly   smarter

clearly   strangest   happier   silliest

trainer   senator   sweetest   teacher

B. Write two words for each suffix. Use the words above.

ly = in a certain manner	or or er = someone who	er = more	est = most

Affixes and Compound Words
Word Study

Practice It!
suffixes
–ly, –or, –er, –est

Name _____

Are You a Word Searcher?

A. Read the words out loud. Circle the suffixes. Share what you think each word means.

| prettier | safer | darker | luckiest | loudly |
| coldest | jogger | quietly | farmer | sailor |

B. Circle the words above in the puzzle. The words can read down, across, or diagonally.

```
C  X  R  J  O  G  G  E  R  R  T
J  O  K  E  U  B  F  D  S  Q  S
Y  T  L  K  I  A  R  Y  A  V  E
L  Z  O  D  R  T  L  Y  I  Y  I
D  F  Q  M  E  T  T  W  L  A  K
U  T  E  P  E  S  H  E  O  M  C
O  R  B  I  G  R  T  L  R  C  U
L  M  U  R  E  K  A  R  D  P  L
N  Q  A  F  I  C  Z  H  Y  Z  E
H  N  A  D  A  R  K  E  R  V  O
H  S  P  P  M  D  G  G  A  H  B
```

C. Write nine of the words you circled.

_____ _____ _____

_____ _____ _____

_____ _____ _____

Review It!

suffixes
–ly, –or, –er, –est

Name _____

Fill in the circle by the word that best completes each sentence.

Desperately Seeking Molly

1. Anya's cat Molly was the _____ cat in the world, but she could be sneaky.

   Ⓐ sweeter Ⓑ sweetest Ⓒ sweetly

2. Molly _____ watched the front door as people went in and out.

   Ⓐ closelyiest Ⓑ closely Ⓒ closer

3. Whenever Molly tried to dash out, Anya would _____ tell her no!

   Ⓐ sternly Ⓑ sternest Ⓒ sterner

4. One rainy day, Molly slipped _____ past Anya's brother Michael.

   Ⓐ quietest Ⓑ quieter Ⓒ quietly

5. "Michael, watch out!" Anya shouted _____, but it was too late.

   Ⓐ loudlier Ⓑ loudly Ⓒ loudest

6. Anya _____ ran out the door and searched for Molly.

   Ⓐ quickest Ⓑ quicker Ⓒ quickly

7. An hour later, Anya _____ found Molly, who was wet and scared.

   Ⓐ finally Ⓑ final Ⓒ finalist

8. Once they were home, Anya fed Molly, wrapped her in a towel, and held her _____ on her lap.

   Ⓐ tightest Ⓑ tightier Ⓒ tightly

Learn It!
suffixes

Name _____

Suffixes: –able, –less, –ness

Every suffix has a meaning.
Knowing the meaning of a suffix can help you figure out the meaning of a word.

able means "can be done" **fixable** means "can be fixed"
less means "without" **careless** means "without care"
ness can mean "the state of" **kindness** means "the state of being kind"

Adding a suffix sometimes changes the spelling of the word.
For most words that end in **y**, change the **y** to **i** and add **ness**.

silly ⟶ silliness

A. Read each word out loud. Circle the suffix. Share what you think each word means.

closeness	climbable	painless	fairness
bendable	pointless	shyness	enjoyable
colorless	sweetness	drinkable	blameless

B. Write three words for each suffix. Use the words above.
Then add your own words to the fourth row.

able = is or can be	less = without	ness = the state of

Practice It!
suffixes
–able, –less, –ness

Name _____

Are You Unbeatable?

A. Read the words out loud. Circle the suffixes. Share what you think each word means.

gentleness	washable	sleepless	happiness
thoughtless	illness	acceptable	useless

B. Write a word from above to match each definition.

1. the state of being happy   _____

2. without thinking of others _____

3. can be cleaned   _____

4. the state of being sick   _____

5. without purpose   _____

6. the state of being gentle   _____

7. without rest   _____

8. is accepted   _____

C. Write a definition for the word *painless*.

_____

_____

Review It!

suffixes
–able, –less, –ness

Name _____

Fill in the circle by the word that best completes each sentence.

Kindness and Care

1. Maria Lopez is known for her _____ to help others.
   - Ⓐ willingness
   - Ⓑ willingless
   - Ⓒ sadness

2. She fixes meals twice a week for _____ people at a shelter.
   - Ⓐ harmness
   - Ⓑ homeless
   - Ⓒ homeness

3. Mrs. Lopez's _____ has won her an award.
   - Ⓐ sadness
   - Ⓑ kindless
   - Ⓒ kindness

4. At the awards dinner, Mrs. Lopez said that many homeless people feel _____.
   - Ⓐ hopeable
   - Ⓑ hopeness
   - Ⓒ hopeless

5. "Everyone is _____ of helping others," she said.
   - Ⓐ capable
   - Ⓑ bendable
   - Ⓒ enjoyable

6. "All efforts make a difference, and no effort is _____."
   - Ⓐ nearness
   - Ⓑ useless
   - Ⓒ friendless

7. "We all can bring some _____ and hope to people who are having hard times."
   - Ⓐ happiness
   - Ⓑ darkness
   - Ⓒ silliness

8. Mrs. Lopez added, "_____ is its own reward."
   - Ⓐ Goodless
   - Ⓑ Goodness
   - Ⓒ Illness

Name _____

Learn It!
compound words

> ## Compound Words
> A compound word is made up of two smaller words.
>
> camp + ground = campground   night + time = nighttime
>
> The two smaller words sometimes give clues to the meaning of the compound word.
>
> goldfish = a fish that's gold
> storyteller = a person who tells stories

A. Read each word out loud. Draw a line between the two words that make up the compound word.

back|ground   himself   outfield   outdoors

rattlesnake   mailbox   daybreak   firefighter

bedroom   cornmeal   notebook   carpool

B. Draw lines to make compound words.

1. ant
2. key
3. sweat
4. fire
5. cow
6. finger
7. side
8. sea

a. works
b. boy
c. shore
d. board
e. ways
f. eater
g. shirt
h. print

Affixes and Compound Words
Word Study

Practice It!
compound words

Name _____

Crossword Time!

A. Read each word out loud. Draw a line between the two words that make the compound word.

popcorn   bulldog   nighttime   cardboard   firefly

haircut   oatmeal   birthday   upstairs   hometown

B. Use words above to complete the crossword puzzle.

Down

1. the time from dusk until dawn
4. up the stairs
5. a strong dog with powerful jaws
6. a snack made of corn

Across

2. a small flying bug that gives off light
3. styled hair
7. a cereal made from oats
8. a stiff paper used to make boxes

Review It!
compound words

Name _____

Fill in the circle by the word that best completes each sentence.

A Family Getaway

1. _____ our family goes away, we hire our friend Ronni to look after our cats.
   - Ⓐ Whatever
   - Ⓑ Whoever
   - Ⓒ Whenever

2. Last weekend, we headed to our favorite _____ and set up our tents.
   - Ⓐ campground
   - Ⓑ campfire
   - Ⓒ runway

3. Before _____, we called Ronni on Mom's cellphone.
   - Ⓐ headlight
   - Ⓑ nighttime
   - Ⓒ seaside

4. Ronni picked up right away and said that it was the cats' _____.
   - Ⓐ overnight
   - Ⓑ watchdog
   - Ⓒ dinnertime

5. "Later on, I'll have them chase the beam from my _____," Ronni said.
   - Ⓐ flashback
   - Ⓑ flashlight
   - Ⓒ firefighter

6. After our call, we watched _____ light up the sky and listened to our headsets.
   - Ⓐ fireflies
   - Ⓑ firewood
   - Ⓒ fireplaces

7. "Let's go hiking after _____ tomorrow morning," I said to mom.
   - Ⓐ background
   - Ⓑ daytime
   - Ⓒ breakfast

8. Mom said that after the hike we could take the _____ out on the lake.
   - Ⓐ seaweed
   - Ⓑ bathtub
   - Ⓒ sailboat

Affixes and Compound Words
Word Study

Read It!

suffixes;
compound words

A Desert Birthday

Amy couldn't be happier. She was spending her birthday with her older brother, Rick. He worked as a park ranger in southeast California. Rick knew that Amy loved the outdoors. So he was taking Amy for a walk in a desert.

They moved easily along the trails. Rick answered Amy's endless questions. He explained that most desert animals had light-colored fur or feathers. The light colors reflected the hot sun instead of soaking it in. Amy thought Rick was the smartest person she knew.

Rick pointed out bighorn sheep and a roadrunner. He said that the roadrunner liked to walk or run rather than fly.

"We're lucky to see these animals. Most desert wildlife moves around at night when it's cooler," said Rick.

"Even rattlesnakes?" asked Amy. Her eyes grew wide. She hated snakes.

"Oh, yeah. Rattlesnakes sense heat. In the nighttime, animals are warmer than their background. So a rattlesnake finds food easily, even in total darkness. Most rattlers are shy. But if you bother them, they'll bite. And their bite is full of poison."

Rick's voice suddenly became demanding. "Stop, Amy!" He grabbed Amy's arm. "Now very slowly move back a step," said Rick. Amy nervously did as she was told.

"Look closely at the ground," said Rick. "See those bumps sticking slightly above the sand? We nearly stepped on a sidewinder snake! It hides in the sand or under rocks in the daytime."

Amy eyes grew wider. Then she smiled and said, "I'm the luckiest person in the world to have a brother like you!"

Apply It!
suffixes;
compound words

Name _____

Now Try This...

1. Look back at the story. Write four words for each suffix.

_____ly	_____er

2. Write four compound words that are used in the story.

   _____   _____

   _____   _____

3. What is unusual about the roadrunner?

   _____

4. Why might Amy feel she is lucky to have a brother like Rick?

   _____

   _____

5. Based on what you read, would you expect a sidewinder to have bright-colored skin?

   _____ Tell why or why not. _____

   _____

6. Practice reading two paragraphs in the story. Then read them to your teacher.

Affixes and Compound Words
Word Study

High-Frequency Words

Overview
High-frequency words are those words in the English language that appear most frequently in print. The purpose of the **High-Frequency Words** section is to give students practice in reading 240 high-frequency words quickly and accurately, thereby helping to develop reading fluency. The word lists on the following pages are compiled from *Dolch Basic Sight Vocabulary* and *Fry's Instant Words*. The high-frequency word lists should be used in tandem with your phonics instruction.

Teaching Tips *pages 268–276*
You may want to use the following steps to review high-frequency words with students:

- Students need one cover (page 268) and all 16 word lists (pages 269–276). Allow time for students to make a booklet by stacking the lists in order with List 1 on top. Have students staple the cover to the word lists along the top, allowing pages to flip back. Once the booklets are made, invite students to skim the lists. Explain why it is important to read the words quickly and accurately. Call attention to the speed drill that follows each list, and establish a procedure for carrying it out. (Students need a partner and a watch with a second hand.) Always allow students additional opportunities to improve their own speed-drill results.

- The word lists allow for flexibility on your part. Use them according to the needs of each struggling reader. There is a benefit to formal instruction, such as the following:

    Read a word out loud, and then use it in a sentence or in several phrases. Write the sentence or phrases on the board, and underline the high-frequency word. Have students tap and spell the word as you point to each letter. Ask students to write the word several times on paper, spelling the word out loud each time it is written.

    Or, have students look at a particular word list and cover half of the words. Say one of the remaining words, and then use it in a sentence or in phrases. Have students point to the word you have said, and then say the word and spell it rhythmically.

Rule Breakers
Reading high-frequency words is a challenge because the words often do not follow the letter/sound relationships that are commonly taught. For example, students struggling to read the word *said* cannot decode by applying the pronunciation of words with the same spelling pattern, such as *maid* and *paid*. Students need to focus on each letter in a high-frequency word or on letter patterns where they occur. Several high-frequency words, for example, begin with the **wh** letter pattern and have the /**wh**/ sound.

High-Frequency Words

Read them fast!

Name _____

High-Frequency Words

Read them fast!

Name _____

List 1

the
to
and
a
I
you
it
in
said
for
up
look
is
go
we

I read _____ words correctly in _____ seconds.

List 2

little
down
can
see
not
one
my
me
big
come
blue
red
where
jump
away

I read _____ words correctly in _____ seconds.

High-Frequency Words
Word Study

List 3

here
help
make
yellow
two
play
run
find
three
funny
he
was
that
she
on

I read _____ words correctly in _____ seconds.

List 4

they
but
at
with
all
there
out
be
have
am
do
did
what
so
get

I read _____ words correctly in _____ seconds.

List 5

like
this
will
yes
went
are
now
no
came
ride
into
good
want
too
pretty

I read _____ words correctly in _____ seconds.

List 6

four
saw
well
ran
brown
eat
who
new
must
black
white
soon
our
ate
say

I read _____ words correctly in _____ seconds.

List 7

under
please
of
his
had
him
her
some
as
then
could
when
were
them
ask

I read _____ words correctly in _____ seconds.

List 8

an
over
just
from
any
how
know
put
take
every
old
by
after
think
let

I read _____ words correctly in _____ seconds.

List 9

going
walk
again
may
stop
fly
round
give
once
open
has
live
thank
boy
day

I read _____ words correctly in _____ seconds.

List 10

man
other
would
very
your
its
around
don't
right
green
their
call
sleep
five
or

I read _____ words correctly in _____ seconds.

List 11

before
been
off
cold
tell
work
first
does
goes
write
always
made
gave
us
buy

I read _____ words correctly in _____ seconds.

List 12

those
use
fast
pull
both
sit
which
read
why
found
wash
because
best
upon
these

I read _____ words correctly in _____ seconds.

List 13

sing
wish
many
also
back
color
each
even
follow
friend
large
last
left
more
most

I read _____ words correctly in _____ seconds.

List 14

near
next
sure
while
way
if
long
about
got
six
never
seven
eight
today
myself

I read _____ words correctly in _____ seconds.

List 15

much
keep
try
start
ten
bring
drink
only
better
hold
warm
full
done
light
pick

I read _____ words correctly in _____ seconds.

List 16

girl
cut
kind
fall
carry
small
own
show
hot
far
draw
woman
grow
together
laugh

I read _____ words correctly in _____ seconds.

Answer Key

Page 11
A. 1. b, 2. a, 3. b, 4. c, 5. a, 6. c
B. 1. a, 2. c, 3. b, 4. b, 5. a, 6. a

Page 12
A. name/nest, dear, take/toss, seven, pen, hot, ring/rude, far, take/toss, name/nest, ring/rude, left

B.

/n/	/r/	/t/
name	ring	take
nest	rude	toss
pen	dear	hot
seven	far	left
Answers will vary in last two rows.		

Page 13
A. name left tail rude ten spot nose dear
B. 1. ten 2. nose 3. left 4. spot
   5. name 6. rude 7. tail 8. dear
C. Answers will vary.

Page 14
A. ladder, band, nail/real, cub/rib, butter, team, list, hum, meat/mess, nail/real, meat/mess, cub/rib

B.

/b/	/l/	/m/
band	ladder	meat
butter	list	mess
cub	nail	hum
rib	real	team
Answers will vary in last two rows.		

Page 15
A. lift mind butter living pencil sum bike main rub mitt
B. 1. ham 2. late 3. rib
   4. baseball 5. bold
   6. mail 7. mother 8. crib
   9. last 10. money

Page 16
1. c 2. b 3. b 4. a
5. a 6. b 7. c 8. b

Page 18
1. Answers will vary.
2. Answers will vary.
3. Mom saw a baseball where a pot once stood. She saw that Mike wore his mitt.
4. Mike wanted to try out his new mitt. Maybe it was raining.
5. The boys should play outside and not in the house.

Page 19
A. 1. c, 2. c, 3. b, 4. a, 5. b, 6. a
B. 1. a, 2. c, 3. a, 4. a, 5. b, 6. c

Page 20
A. elf, farm, dash/duck, part/push, help, cold/herd, fence, cold/herd, dash/duck, sheep, part/push, leaf

B.

/d/	/f/	/p/
dash	farm	part
duck	fence	push
cold	elf	help
herd	leaf	sheep
Answers will vary in last two rows.		

Page 21
A. fact shelf farm dash part stamp bold sheep
B. 1. farm 2. sheep 3. part
   4. shelf 5. fact
C. stamp

Page 22
A. keep/king, hang/head/herd/hope, five/love, visit, fork, vase, snack

B.

/h/	/k/	/v/
hang	keep	vase
head	king	visit
herd	fork	five
hope	snack	love
Answers will vary in last two rows.		

Page 23
A. king glove snack visit hang kite herding vase
B. **Across**
   1. snack
   5. vase
   7. herding
   8. king
   Down
   2. kite
   3. glove
   4. hang
   6. visit

Page 24
1. a 2. c 3. b 4. c
5. c 6. b 7. b 8. a

Page 26
1. Answers will vary.
2. Answers will vary.
3. He lived in the city and might never have been on a horse. He always wanted to ride a horse.
4. Answers will vary.
5. Answers will vary.

Page 27
A. 1. c, 2. b, 3. b, 4. a, 5. b, 6. c
B. 1. b, 2. a, 3. a, 4. c, 5. a, 6. c

Page 28
A. jade/joke/jump/just, yak/yes, wild/wish/woke, water, year/your

B.

/j/	/w/	/y/
jade	water	yak
joke	wild	yes
jump	wish	year
just	woke	your
Answers will vary in last two rows.		

Page 29
A. jade yell joke wings yellow walrus yard jumping
B. 1. joke 2. yard 3. jade
   4. wings 5. walrus
   6. jumping 7. yellow 8. yell
C. Answers will vary.

Page 30
A.

/kw/	/ks/	/z/
queen	ax	size
quick	box	zero
quite	fix	zebra
question	mix	froze

B.

/kw/	/ks/	/z/
queen	ax	size
quick	box	zero
quite	fix	zebra
question	mix	froze

Page 31

A.

/ks/	fixed	boxer	mix
/z/	zone	size	zebra
/kw/	quilt	quick	quit

B.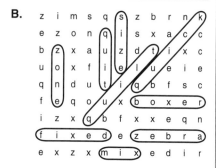

C. Words match those circled in the puzzle on the page and may be written in any order.

Page 32
1. c   2. a   3. b   4. c
5. a   6. b   7. c   8. a

Page 33
A.
B. 1. class, press, toss
   2. dull, wall; Answers will vary.
   3. egg, odd
   4. puff/stiff/stuff, fizz/fuzz

Page 34
A.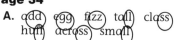
B. 1. ll, 2. ss, 3. ll, 4. zz, 5. ff,
   6. ff, 7. dd, 8. ll, 9. ll, 10. ss

Page 35
1. c   2. b   3. a   4. a
5. b   6. c   7. c   8. a

Page 37
1. Answers will vary.
2. Answers will vary.
3. Answers will vary, such as: to show they are smart; to win a prize for their school; to take on a challenge.
4. Answers will vary, such as: Jess wasn't prepared because she had replaced Jade. Jess was scared. Jess didn't get to practice.
5. Answers will vary, such as: Jade, the girl Jess replaced, was sick with the flu.

Page 39
1. a   2. d   3. b   4. c
5. b   6. a   7. c   8. d

Page 40
A. Sam **S**, same **L**, fake **L**, stand **S**, fade **L**, black **S**, brand **S**, last **S**, plan **S**, plane **L**, plate **L**, trade **L**

B.

short *a*	long *a*
black	fade
brand	fake
last	plane
plan	plate
Sam	same
stand	trade
Answers will vary in last three rows.	

Page 41
A. rabbit **S**, snakes **L**, plan **S**, cage **L**, cape **L**, cap **S**, plane **L**, tame **L**
B. 1. cap, 2. snakes, 3. cape, 4. rabbit, 5. cage, 6. plan, 7. tame, 8. plane
C. Answers will vary.

Page 42
1. b   2. c   3. b   4. c
5. a   6. b   7. a   8. a

Page 43
A. bent **S**, chess **S**, teeth **LL**, sent **S**, fed **S**, feed **LL**, bled **S**, bleed **LL**, sleep **LL**, maybe **L**, pet **S**, three **LL**

B.

short *e*	long *e*
bent	bleed
bled	feed
chess	maybe
fed	sleep
pet	teeth
sent	three
Answers will vary in last three rows.	

Page 44
A. queen **LL**, sheep **LL**, bed **S**, sleep **LL**, sent **S**, cent **S**, tent **S**, shed **S**
B. sent, cent, tent, shed, bed, sleep, sheep, queen
C. green

Page 45
1. b   2. c   3. b   4. c
5. a   6. b   7. c   8. a

Page 46
A. rip **S**, ripe **L**, drip **S**, skin **S**, still **S**, mist **S**, grind **L**, spice **L**, dim **S**, dime **L**, line **L**, mile **L**

B.

short *i*	long *i*
dim	dime
drip	grind
mist	line
rip	mile
skin	ripe
still	spice
Answers will vary in last three rows.	

Page 47
A. smile **L**, ship **S**, fish **S**, dim **S**, slide **L**, dime **L**, swim **S**, rip **S**, bike **L**, skip **S**
B. 1. b   2. d   3. g   4. h
   5. f   6. a   7. c   8. e
C. Answers will vary.

Page 48
1. b   2. a   3. c   4. a
5. c   6. b   7. b   8. c

Page 50
1. Answers will vary.
2. Answers will vary, such as: Amber wasn't old enough to care for a pet.
3. Rabbits are destructive and eat wires and wood. Amber's parents would be mad.
4. Answers will vary, such as: A lizard is quiet, eats little, and won't destroy the furniture.

Page 51
A. 1. d   2. a   3. c   4. b   5. a
B. 1. d   2. c   3. c

Page 52
A. broke **L**, dock **S**, alone **L**, clothes **L**, pond **S**, rock **S**, code **L**, shop **S**, shock **S**, globe **L**, plot **S**, zero **L**

B.

short *o*	long *o*
dock	alone
plot	broke
pond	clothes
rock	code
shock	globe
shop	zero
Answers will vary in last three rows.	

Page 53
A. crops **S**, broken **L**, mop **S**, shock **S**, hero **L**, omit **L**, mope **L**, robe **L**, pond **S**, smoke **L**
B. 1. mop, 2. broken, 3. mope, 4. hero, 5. crops, 6. omit, 7. pond, 8. smoke
C. Answers will vary.

Page 54
1. c 2. b 3. b 4. c
5. a 6. c 7. a 8. c

Page 55
A. cub **S**, cube **L**, gum **S**, blue **L**, hug **S**, huge **L**, flute **L**, upset **S**, menu **L**, dust **S**, clump **S**, usual **LL**

B.
short *u*	long *u*
clump	blue
cub	cube
dust	flute
gum	huge
hug	menu
upset	usual
Answers will vary in last three rows.	

Page 56
A. dunk **S**, dust **S**, fume **L**, brush **S**, bump **S**, cut **S**, hug **S**, Luke **L**, tube **L**, unless **S**

B. 1. d 2. h 3. f 4. c
5. e 6. a 7. b 8. g

C. Answers will vary.

Page 57
1. b 2. c 3. b 4. b
5. a 6. c 7. b 8. b

Page 58
A. silly **E**, shy **I**, dry **I**, muddy **E**, anyone **E**, body **E**, sunny **E**, candy **E**, try **I**, type **I**, reply **I**, spy **I**

B.
y as long *e*	*y* as long *i*
anyone	dry
body	reply
candy	shy
muddy	spy
silly	try
sunny	type
Answers will vary in last three rows.	

Page 59
A. puppy **E**, fly **I**, anytime **E**, muddy **E**, why **I**, body **E**, silly **E**, bury **E**, shy **I**, happy **E**

B. **Down**
1. fly
2. happy
4. muddy
6. shy
7. bury

Across
3. anytime
5. body
6. silly
8. puppy
9. why

Page 60
1. b 2. a 3. b 4. c
5. c 6. a 7. b 8. a

Page 62
1. Answers will vary.
2. The weather was cold and probably snowy.
3. Answers will vary, such as: People today wear fur clothes and leg warmers. People still hunt for food. People eat nuts, berries, and meat.
4. Answers will vary.

Page 63
A. 1. b 2. c 3. a 4. c
B. 1. b 2. a 3. b
C. 1. a 2. b 3. c 4. b

Page 64
A. (sip) (mug) (fad) (nut) (wet) (nod) (sob) (fix) (men) (tab)
All the vowel sounds are short.
B. short
C. Answers will vary.

Page 65
A. cvc dab, cvc rot, cvc sob, cvc hip, cvc hem, cvc lug, cvc map, cvc tin, cvc net, cvc cut
B. 1. u, 2. a, 3. i, 4. i, 5. e, 6. o, 7. u, 8. o
C. Answers will vary.

Page 66
1. c 2. a 3. c 4. b
5. a 6. b 7. a 8. c

Page 67
A. cvcc dent, cvcc hand, cvcc lump, cvcc mask, cvcc bond, cvcc left, cvcc just, cvcc soft, cvcc lift, cvcc miss, cvcc lint, cvcc sent
B. short
C. Answers will vary.

Page 68
A. cvcc gift, cvcc send, cvcc lung, cvcc fond, cvcc task, cvcc belt, cvcc bent, cvcc rust
B. 1. hand, 2. wolf, 3. begs, 4. lick, 5. pant, 6. mutt, 7. kiss, 8. help
C. I can send a gift.

Page 69
1. c 2. a 3. c 4. b
5. a 6. c 7. b 8. c

Page 70
A. cvc wave✗, cvc pole✗, cvc cute✗, cvc dive✗, cvc note✗, cvc hide✗, cvc fade✗, cvc save✗, cvc cube✗, cvc cone✗, cvc time✗, cvc tale✗
B. long
C. Answers will vary.

Page 71
A. cvc nice✗, cvc cube✗, cvc same✗, cvc vase✗, cvc ripe✗, cvc cave✗, cvc lake✗, cvc bone✗
B. **Down**
1. cube
2. bone
3. vase
5. cave

Across
4. nice
6. same
7. lake
8. ripe

Page 72
1. a 2. c 3. c 4. b
5. c 6. b 7. a 8. b

Page 74
1.
CVC	CVCC	CVCe
Ben	back	game
hid	bent	nine
tub	gasp	vase
tug		

2. Answers will vary, such as: Yes. They played with Luke. Yes. They asked for a story.
3. Answers will vary, such as: The boys ran off.
4. Answers will vary, such as: Luke bribed the boys with a treat.

Page 76
1. a, 2. b, 3. a, 4. b, 5. b, 6. c, 7. c, 8. a, 9. c, 10. b, 11. a, 12. b

Page 77
A.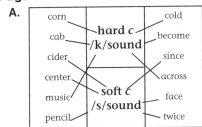

B. Answers will vary.

Page 78

A. k   s   k   s   s
cash   city   corn   office   since

s   k   s   k   k
decide candy dance cupcake code

B. 1. dance, 2. corn, 3. candy,
4. decide, 5. cash, 6. office,
7. code, 8. city

C. Answers will vary.

Page 79

1. a 2. c 3. b 4. a
5. b 6. c 7. c 8. b

Page 80

A.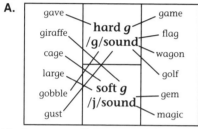

B. Answers will vary.

Page 81

A. j   g   g   g   g
giraffe began goldfish gap gate

j   j   g   g   j
page giant gulf garden gentle

B. 1. c 2. e 3. g 4. f
5. a 6. h 7. d 8. b

C. Answers will vary.

Page 82

1. a 2. c 3. c 4. b
5. c 6. a 7. b 8. a

Page 83

A.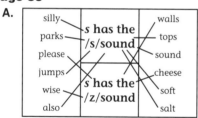

B. Answers will vary.

Page 84

A. z   s   z   s   s
rise save molds salt sing

z   z   s   s   z
walls watches soft pants runs

B.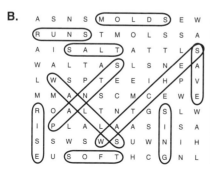

C. Accept any nine words that match the circled words in the puzzle.

Page 85

1. a 2. b 3. b 4. c
5. a 6. c 7. b 8. c

Page 87

1. Answers will vary.
2. Morgan does not have much willpower.
3. Answers will vary.
4. Answers will vary.

Page 88

1. b 2. a 3. c 4. c
5. c 6. a 7. c 8. b 9. a

Page 89

A. bench, whale, whisper, shark, wheel, thin, fish, shape, child, gather, math, rich

B.
ch	sh	th	wh
bench	fish	gather	whale
child	shape	math	wheel
rich	shark	thin	whisper
Answers will vary in last two rows.			

Page 90

A. finish, whale, chase, thunder, white, whisper, thirty, shapes, nothing, cash

B. **Down**
1. whale
2. whisper
4. thirty
5. nothing
6. shapes

Across
3. white
4. thunder
7. finish
8. chase

Page 91

1. b 2. a 3. c 4. c
5. a 6. c 7. a 8. b

Page 92

A. photo, telephone, rough, phase, laugh, cough, alphabet, tough, enough, graph, laughter, trophy

B.
ph spells the /f/ sound	gh spells the /f/ sound
alphabet	cough
graph	enough
phase	laugh
photo	laughter
telephone	rough
trophy	tough

Page 93

A. enough, elephant, photos, tough, phone, rough, cough, alphabet

B. 1. cough, 2. phone, 3. elephant,
4. photos, 5. rough, 6. alphabet,
7. tough, 8. enough

C. laughter

Page 94

1. a 2. a 3. c 4. b
5. c 6. b 7. b 8. c

Page 96

1. Answers will vary.
2. Answers will vary, such as: Barnacles attach themselves to gray whales. Gray whales have no top fin. Gray whales have a double blowhole. The gray whale's fluke has a notch down the middle. The gray whale's spout looks like a heart.
3. My nose and nostrils help me breathe.
4. Answers will vary.

Page 97

1. b 2. b 3. c 4. a 5. b
6. b 7. a 8. c 9. b 10. a

Page 98

A.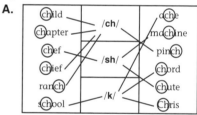

B.
/ch/	/sh/	/k/
chapter	chef	ache
chief	chute	chord
child	machine	Chris
pinch		school
ranch		

Page 99

A. sh   ch   ch   k   ch
machine children chase stomach lunch

ch   k   ch   ch   sh
sandwich school branch chimps chef

B. 1. stomach, 2. chef, 3. branch,
4. lunch, 5. sandwich, 6. chimps,
7. chase, 8. children

C. Answers will vary.

Page 100

1. c 2. b 3. c 4. a
5. c 6. a 7. b 8. c

Page 101

A. special addition station
   delicious rushed action
   subtraction share motion
   flashing social clash

B.

sh - /sh/	ci - /sh/	ti - /sh/
clash	delicious	action
flashing	social	addition
rushed	special	motion
share		station
		subtraction

Page 102

A. action trash fiction special
   shin addition rushed
   delicious motion share

B. **Down**
1. shin
3. delicious
4. trash
5. motion

Across
2. addition
6. fiction
7. special
8. rushed

Page 103

1. c 2. c 3. a 4. b
5. c 6. c 7. a 8. b

Page 105

1. ache ached anchors
   chemicals Chris school
   stomach

2.
ti	action motion nation pollution
ci	delicious special

3. Answers will vary, such as: responsible, caring
4. Answers will vary, such as: the environment; their muscles.
5. Answers will vary.

Page 107

1. cr   4. fr   7. tr   10. pr
2. bl   5. gl   8. cl   11. fl
3. pl   6. br   9. gr   12. br

Page 108

A. broke cry trick pride fresh
   grade brand grab crash drag
   trade drive press Friday treat

B.

br__	dr__	gr__	pr__	tr__
brand	drag	grab	press	trade
broke	drive	grade	pride	treat
				trick

Answers will vary in last two rows.

Page 109

A. brush crate drive press
   crab pride tracks frame
   grades Friday

B. 1. c 2. g 3. d 4. i 5. b
   6. e 7. h 8. a 9. f 10. j

C. Answers will vary.

Page 110

1. b 2. a 3. b 4. c
5. a 6. c 7. b 8. a

Page 111

A. class block flip plate
   blimp planet globe plum
   flash flame bleed clap
   clam glide glance

B.

bl__	cl__	fl__	gl__	pl__
bleed	clam	flame	glance	planet
blimp	clap	flash	glide	plate
block	class	flip	globe	plum

Answers will vary in last two rows.

Page 112

A. planet Club class Please
   plan glance play glad
   block blanket

B. planet, Club, play, Please, class, plan, block, glad

Page 113

1. b 2. c 3. c 4. b
5. a 6. c 7. b 8. a

Page 115

1. Answers will vary.
2. Answers will vary, such as: The people ate food. The people played music and sang. The people decorated.
3. Answers will vary, such as: Crista didn't want Tracy to think her family was weird.
4. Answers will vary, such as: Crista was proud to be in a family that cared about each other.

Page 116

1. sn   5. sw   9. ft
2. sk   6. nd   10. st
3. sp   7. nk
4. st   8. nt

Page 117

A. stop sleeve sting slide
   skill spell skate swing
   smoke snack stack swim
   skim speed smart

B.

sl__	sm__	sp__	st__	sw__
sleeve	smart	speed	stack	swim
slide	smoke	spell	sting	swing
			stop	

Answers will vary in last row.

Page 118

A. swing stick skating snip
   sleeve step smoke spelling

B.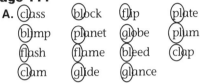

C. Words match those circled in the puzzle on the page and may be written in any order.

Page 119

1. c 2. b 3. a 4. b
5. c 6. a 7. b 8. c

Page 120

A. blank plant rest left
   bend blend swift past
   hint mild trunk clump
   brand gold camp

B.

__ft	__ld	__nk	__nt	__st
left	gold	blank	hint	past
swift	mild	trunk	plant	rest

Answers will vary in last row.

Page 121

A. mist drink blend ring
   skunk blimp west gold
   invent drift

B. 1. hand 2. contest 3. cold
   4. pint 5. bald 6. crust
   7. absent 8. mind

C. Answers will vary.

Page 122

1. c 2. a 3. b 4. b
5. c 6. a 7. c 8. b

Page 124

1. Answers will vary.
2. Answers will vary, such as: It was beginning to snow, so Stella wanted to take the shortest path back to her grandparents.
3. Answers will vary, such as: Skipper would have dragged Stella out. Skipper would have rushed to Stella's grandparents and led them to the pond.
4. Answers will vary, such as: Stella's sleeping bag. The sleeping bag is soft and keeps Stella warm.

Page 126
A. 1. d 2. b 3. a 4. d 5. c
B. 1. b 2. d 3. a 4. b 5. d

Page 127
A. steak trailer remain prey freeway tray hey outbreak obey always paid great

B.
Long a spelled ai	Long a spelled ay	Long a spelled ea	Long a spelled ey
paid	always	great	hey
remain	freeway	outbreak	obey
trailer	tray	steak	prey

Page 128
A. sailboat subway prey mayor brain daybreak obey Milky Way afraid steak

B. 1. subway, 2. sailboat, 3. brain, 4. steak, 5. prey, 6. daybreak, 7. Milky Way, 8. obey, 9. afraid, 10. mayor

C. Answers will vary.

Page 129
1. c 2. a 3. b 4. c
5. c 6. a 7. c 8. b

Page 130
A. teeth donkey feet yield money chief dream honey beak needle meal believe

B.
Long e spelled ea	Long e spelled ee	Long e spelled ey	Long e spelled ie
beak	feet	donkey	believe
dream	needle	honey	chief
meal	teeth	money	yield
Answers will vary in last row.			

Page 131
A. needle meat donkey shield wheat cookie money creep sweet beads

B.
```
H C C R N E E D L E H
C O O K I S D T W A E
N H T O D T E A W H B
H E E A K T Y S H B E
  C R E E P   I H E A
D B T L T E E E M A D
O I T A I D M I L R S
N E E U L O R E C C
K M B I N T R D L W R
E O H E H A D A N K E
Y S Y W E S W E E T T
```

C. Accept any nine words that match the circled words in the puzzle.

Page 132
1. a 2. c 3. c 4. b
5. a 6. c 7. c 8. b

Page 134
1. Answers will vary.
2. a. moray eel   c. sea star
   b. sea horse   d. sea snail
3. Answers will vary, such as: A moray eel could sting you with the spines on its tail.
4. Answers will vary.

Page 135
A. 1. b 2. c 3. a 4. b
B. 1. d 2. c 3. a
C. 1. b 2. c 3. a

Page 136
A. dye buy guys rye night lye lie high sigh bright died pie

B.
Long i spelled ie	Long i spelled igh	Long i spelled uy	Long i spelled ye
died	bright	buy	dye
lie	high	guys	lye
pie	night		rye
	sigh		

Page 137
A. pie right buys dye lie light guy rye sigh highlight

B. 1. e 2. d 3. a 4. g 5. b
6. c 7. h 8. f 9. j 10. i

C. Answers will vary.

Page 138
1. c 2. b 3. b 4. c
5. a 6. b 7. b 8. c

Page 139
A. thrown soap doe float toe follow slowly boast crow foe oak Joe

B.
Long o spelled oa	Long o spelled oe	Long o spelled ow
boast	doe	crow
float	foe	follow
oak	Joe	slowly
soap	toe	thrown
Answers will vary in last row.		

Page 140
A. window stows float doe toast tows soap slowly yellow woes

B. **Down**
1. yellow
3. stows
4. woes
6. tows
7. float

Across
2. toast
4. window
5. doe
8. slowly
9. soap

Page 141
1. c 2. c 3. b 4. a
5. a 6. c 7. b 8. b

Page 142
A. grew cue true threw news crew few clue fuel hue argue jewel

B.
Long u spelled ew	Long u spelled ue
crew	argue
few	clue
grew	cue
jewel	fuel
news	hue
threw	true

Page 143
A. value glue overdue clues untrue news renew chew

B. 1. untrue 2. chew 3. clues
4. renew 5. glue
6. overdue 7. news

C. Answers will vary.

Page 144
1. a 2. c 3. c 4. b
5. b 6. c 7. a 8. b

Page 146
1. Answers will vary.
2. Answers will vary.
3. Answers will vary, such as: At first, Joe was disappointed when his family didn't mention his birthday. Then, Joe was happy when his family and friends surprised him.
4. Answers will vary.

Page 147
1. b 2. c 3. b 4. a 5. c
6. b 7. a 8. a 9. b 10. c

Page 148
A. thread buildings rough ready young meadow country guilt instead touch spread enough

B.
Short e spelled ea	Short i spelled ui	Short u spelled ou
instead	buildings	country
meadow	guilt	enough
ready		rough
spread		touch
thread		young

Page 149
A. enough build spread ready country already Instead tough

B. enough, build, already, tough, spread, ready, country, Instead

Page 150
1. a 2. b 3. c 4. c
5. b 6. c 7. b 8. a

Page 151
A.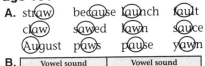

B.
Vowel sound spelled *au*	Vowel sound spelled *aw*
August	claw
because	lawn
fault	paws
launch	sawed
pause	straw
sauce	yawn

Page 152
A.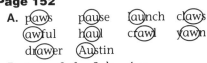

B. 1. e 2. f 3. h 4. c
   5. d 6. g 7. b 8. a
C. Answers will vary.

Page 153
1. b 2. a 3. c 4. b
5. a 6. b 7. c 8. c

Page 155
1. Answers will vary.
2.
/ui/ short *i*	guilty	guinea pig
/ou/ short *u*	cousin	young

3. Answers will vary, such as: Heather's imagination was stirred by the mysterious scratching sounds.
4. Answers will vary.
5. Answers will vary, such as: The guinea pig came out of hiding when it smelled the bread.

Page 156
1. c 2. a 3. b 4. c
5. a 6. b 7. c 8. b

Page 157
A.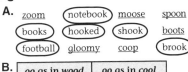

B.
oo as in *wood*	oo as in *cool*
books	boots
brook	coop
football	gloomy
hooked	moose
notebook	spoon
shook	zoom
Answers will vary in last row.	

Page 158
A.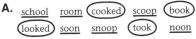

B. school, book, cooked, scoop, noon, room

Page 159
1. b 2. c 3. a 4. c
5. b 6. b 7. a 8. a

Page 160
A.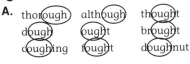

B.
Long *o* as in *though*	Short *o* as in *cough*
although	brought
dough	coughing
doughnut	fought
thorough	ought
	thought

Page 161
A.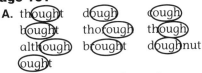

B. 1. **th**ought   5. **b**rought
   2. **d**ough   6. **thor**ough
   3. **c**ough   7. **dough**nut
   4. **th**ough   8. **b**ough**t**

Page 162
1. c 2. a 3. b 4. a
5. c 6. c 7. c 8. b

Page 164
1. Answers will vary.
2. dough; coughed/thought
3. Answers will vary.
4. Answers will vary.
5. Answers will vary, such as: The title seems to say that Ryan could not make a mistake.

Page 166
1. a 2. b 3. b 4. a 5. c
6. b 7. c 8. a 9. b 10. a

Page 167
A.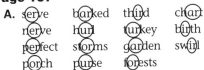

B.
ar	or	er	ir	ur
barked	forests	nerve	birth	hurl
chart	porch	perfect	swirl	purse
garden	storms	serve	third	turkey
Answers will vary in last row.				

Page 168
A.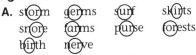

B. 1. purse 2. farms 3. germs
   4. surf   5. skirts 6. forests
   7. storm 8. birth
C. Answers will vary.

Page 169
1. b 2. c 3. b 4. c
5. c 6. a 7. a 8. b

Page 171
1. Answers will vary.
2. A tornado is a powerful wind that swirls and spins.
3. A waterspout forms over water and is weaker than a tornado.
4. Answers will vary.

Page 173
1. ha/l/f, 2. r/h/yme, 3. of/t/en,
4. clim/b/, 5. /k/nob, 6. /g/nat, 7. s/c/ene,
8. /w/rapped, 9. dou/b/t, 10. lis/t/en,
11. wa/l/k, 12. fas/t/en, 13. /k/nee,
14. thum/b/, 15. si/g/n, 16. s/c/ent

Page 174
A. /h/our   ta/l/k   o/h/
   /h/onest yo/l/k T/h/omas
   cha/l/k   rhino   /h/onor
   fo/l/ks   wa/l/k ha/l/f

B.
Silent *h*	Silent *l*
honest	chalk
honor	folks
hour	half
oh	talk
rhino	walk
Thomas	yolk

Page 175
A. /h/erb   cha/l/k   g/h/ost   sta/l/ks
   r/h/yme sa/l/mon /h/onor   yo/l/k
   r/h/ino fo/l/ks

B. **Across**
   1. chalk
   4. rhino
   7. yolk
   8. salmon
   Down
   2. herb
   3. folks
   5. stalks
   6. honor

Page 176
1. a 2. c 3. b 4. c
5. a 6. b 7. b 8. c

Page 177

A. ca**s**tle s**c**ent s**c**ented sof**t**en
   lis**t**en s**c**issors glis**t**en s**c**ene
   whis**t**le s**c**ience s**c**ientist fas**t**en

B.
Silent *t*	Silent *c*
castle	scene
fasten	scent
glisten	scented
listen	science
soften	scientist
whistle	scissors

Page 178

A. fas**t**en s**c**ent whis**t**le glis**t**ens
   cas**t**le s**c**ience s**c**ientist
   lis**t**ening s**c**enery s**c**issors

B. 1. d   2. g   3. i   4. f   5. b
   6. a   7. j   8. c   9. h   10. e

C. Answers will vary.

Page 179

1. c   2. a   3. b   4. a
5. c   6. a   7. c   8. c

Page 180

A. **k**neel **g**nome **k**nob **k**nit
   gnat **k**nock si**g**n desi**g**n
   knot assi**g**n **k**nack **g**nash

B.
Silent *g*	Silent *k*
assign	knack
design	kneel
gnash	knit
gnat	knob
gnome	knock
sign	knot

Page 181

A. **k**neecap si**g**n **k**nuckle **k**nots
   desi**g**n **k**nock **g**nat assi**g**n
   gnash **k**neel

B. 1. kneel, 2. knots, 3. assign,
   4. gnat, 5. kneecap, 6. design,
   7. knock, 8. sign

C. knights

Page 182

1. c   2. a   3. b   4. b
5. a   6. b   7. b   8. b

Page 183

A. **w**reck com**b** **w**ring **w**riting
   thum**b** **w**rong lim**b** **w**rist
   num**b** lam**b** ans**w**er dou**b**t

B.
Silent *b*	Silent *w*
comb	answer
doubt	wreck
lamb	wring
limb	wrist
numb	writing
thumb	wrong

Page 184

A. **w**rapper **w**rong plum**b**er lim**b**s
   wrist **w**rinkle thum**b** ans**w**er
   dou**b**t crum**b**

B. 1. wrapper, 2. doubt, 3. thumb,
   4. answer, 5. wrong, 6. limbs,
   7. wrist, 8. wrinkle

C. Answers will vary.

Page 185

1. c   2. b   3. a   4. c
5. b   6. a   7. c   8. b

Page 187

1. Answers will vary.
2. stalks, calf
3. Answers will vary.
4. Answers will vary, such as: mad or grumpy
5. Answers will vary, such as: Cody told Carlos not to worry about the fish nibbling his knee. Cody stood by Carlos on the ridge.

Page 189

A. 1. b, 2. d, 3. b, 4. a, 5. c, 6. a
B. 1. d, 2. b, 3. c, 4. d, 5. a, 6. c

Page 190

A. br**oi**l destr**oy** p**oi**nt t**oy**s
   enj**oy** sp**oi**l j**oy**ful ann**oy**
   av**oi**d j**oi**ned l**oy**al n**oi**se

B.
/oi/ spelled *oi*	/oi/ spelled *oy*
avoid	annoy
broil	destroy
joined	enjoy
noise	joyful
point	loyal
spoil	toys

Answers will vary in last row.

Page 191

A. g**ow**n d**ow**nt**ow**n sc**ou**t
   eyebr**ow** d**ou**bt sh**ou**t
   someh**ow** gr**ow**l am**ou**nt
   dr**ow**n b**ou**nd cl**ou**d

B.
/ow/ spelled *ow*	/ow/ spelled *ou*
downtown	amount
drown	bound
eyebrow	cloud
gown	doubt
growl	scout
somehow	shout

Answers will vary in last row.

Page 192

A. c**ou**nt dr**ow**n m**oi**st n**oi**sy
   b**ou**nded ann**oy** gr**ow**l t**ow**n
   someh**ow** empl**oy**

B.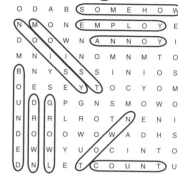

C. Accept any nine words that match the circled words in the puzzle.

Page 193

1. b   2. c   3. b   4. a
5. c   6. b   7. b   8. c

Page 195

1. Answers will vary.
2. Troy, shouted, Scout, chow, choice, bounded, howling, boy, now
3. Troy wanted to lure Scout to him.
4. Scout came to Troy rather than grab the steak off the grill.
5. Answers will vary.

Page 197

A. 1. 2, 2   2. 2, 2   3. 2, 2
   4. 2, 2   5. 1, 1   6. 3, 3

B. 1. b, 2. b, 3. a, 4. a, 5. b, 6. a

Page 198

A.
	Vowel Sounds	Syllables
sudden	2	2
absent	2	2
profile	2	2
cabin	2	2
cactus	2	2
common	2	2
moment	2	2
subject	2	2
habitat	3	3
secret	2	2

B. mo<u>ment</u>, <u>sud</u>den, com<u>mon</u>, <u>ab</u>sent, cac<u>tus</u>, <u>pro</u>file, ca<u>bin</u>, habi<u>tat</u>

Page 199

A. cab|in med|al Chi|na
   vel|vet of|fice prac|tice
   lo|cal at|las spi|der
   ab|sent

B. 1. d, office   5. f, absent
   2. e, local   6. b, velvet
   3. a, medal   7. h, spider
   4. g, China   8. c, atlas

Page 200

1. b 2. c 3. a 4. c
5. c 6. a 7. b 8. c

Page 201

A. plat|ter hur|ried clap|ping
   car|ry pud|dle zip|per lit|ter
   pil|low fel|low hum|ming
   bud|dy com|mon

B. 1. pad|dle 2. shal|low
   3. slip|per 4. hid|den
   5. rug|ged 6. pep|per
   7. gig|gle 8. vil|lage

Page 202

A. but|ter pad|dle mam|mals
   shop|ping hap|py fol|lows
   fos|sil run|ning pud|dles
   hum|ming

B. 1. shopping, 2. puddles,
   3. mammals, 4. paddle,
   5. butter, 6. fossil,
   7. follows, 8. humming

C. middle

Page 203

1. c 2. a 3. c 4. b
5. c 6. a 7. b 8. c

Page 205

1. Answers will vary.
2. de|vice a|gent la|ser
   of|fice won|dered
3. Answers will vary.
4. Answers will vary.
5. Luke was tangled in the sheets.

Page 206

A. 1. a|lone 3. com|bine 5. com|mon
   2. cac|tus 4. pro|file 6. po|lice

B. 1. b 2. c 3. a 4. d
C. 1. d 2. a
D. 1. b 2. c

Page 207

B. a|lert a|bout a|bove
   a|head a|loud di|vide
   po|lice a|fraid de|gree
   a|gainst

Page 208

A. against alone combine
   correct degree pajamas
   potato divide polite
   complete

B. 1. f 2. e 3. d 4. g
   5. h 6. b 7. c 8. a

C. Answers will vary.

Page 209

1. c 2. b 3. a 4. b
5. c 6. c 7. b 8. a

Page 210

A. margin cable human local
   simple title raisin gerbil
   bacon lemon nickel happen

B.
schwa + /n/ sound	schwa + /l/ sound
bacon	cable
happen	gerbil
human	local
lemon	nickel
margin	simple
raisin	title

Page 211

A. person castle candle cousin
   middle dozen slogan lemon
   final cable

B. 1. castle 2. dozen 3. middle
   4. candle 5. cousin 6. cable
   7. lemon 8. person

C. Answers will vary.

Page 212

1. a 2. c 3. b 4. b
5. c 6. b 7. a 8. c

Page 213

A. sugar differ motor chapter
   temper harbor collar mayor
   feather solar bother cellar

B. solar temper collar
   mayor sugar harbor
   motor differ chapter
   cellar bother feather

Page 214

A. doctor tender ladder flavor
   lunar mayor lobster solar
   temper chapter

B. **Across**
   1. lunar
   2. doctor
   6. lobster
   7. mayor

   Down
   1. ladder
   3. chapter
   4. flavor
   5. solar

Page 215

1. b 2. b 3. a 4. c
5. b 6. c 7. a 8. c

Page 217

1. Answers will vary.
2. Lauren's dog Mabel pushed Lauren out of bed.
3. Probably not, because Lauren could feel Mabel pushing against her back.
4. Answers will vary, such as: oversleeping; set her alarm.

Page 220

A. 1. b 2. c 3. b 4. a 5. c
B. 1. b 2. a 3. c 4. c 5. b

Page 221

A. planets lobbies foxes valleys
   countries brushes cities glasses
   watches dreams jackets benches

B. hours candies parties
   speeches trays mixes
   boxes dishes masks

Page 222

A. puppies monkeys boxes matches
   brushes parents artists pockets
   houses classes

B.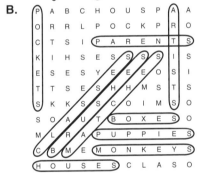

C. Accept any nine words that match the circled words in the puzzle.

Page 223

1. a 2. b 3. b 4. c
5. a 6. c 7. b 8. c

Page 224

A. fish moose shrimp leaves
   teeth geese loaves wolves
   women shelves sheep mice

B.
Plural	
moose	geese
shelves	mice
teeth	shrimp
loaves	fish
sheep	wolves
women	leaves

Page 225
A. wives bacon (children) leaves
shrimp (women) knives wheat
(feet) scarves
B. 1. j 2. c 3. g 4. b 5. i
6. a 7. f 8. h 9. e 10. d
C. Answers will vary.

Page 226
1. b 2. b 3. b 4. c
5. a 6. c 7. b 8. b

Page 227
A. (spied) (worried) (tried)
burying (wrapped) shopped
adding (traded) shopping
(danced) changing (wanted)

B.
Add –ed	Add –ing
cried	crying
melted	melting
bragged	bragging
denied	denying
tasted	tasting
nodded	nodding

Page 228
A. (adding) danced (shopping)
melted tried spied
bragged wanted (denying)
(trading)

B. **Down**
1. bragged
2. adding
4. trading
6. spied

Across
3. wanted
5. danced
7. shopping
8. tried

Page 229
1. c 2. a 3. b 4. b
5. a 6. c 7. a 8. c

Page 230
Past Form
threw
thought
slept
went
had
sang
was
were
broke
caught

Page 231
A. 1. e 2. g 3. c 4. b
5. h 6. d 7. f 8. a
B. Answers will vary.

Page 232
1. b 2. c 3. b 4. a
5. c 6. b 7. a 8. c

Page 234
1.
Plurals Nouns	Verbs - Irregular Past Form	Verbs - Regular Past Form
children	saw	stopped
shelves	broke	begged
sizes	said	spied
mysteries		

2. They couldn't find a gift that both of their parents would like.
3. Answers will vary.
4. Answers will vary, such as: Sam and Maya are considerate. They spend their time finding just the right gift for their parents.

Page 236
A. 1. a, 2. b, 3. a, 4. c, 5. a, 6. c
B. 1. a, 2. c, 3. b, 4. a, 5. c

Page 237
A. (spider's) brothers' women's
(bird's) children's (door's)
countries' coaches' shoes'
(Marie's) sailors' (city's)

B. spider's spiders' child's
children's girl's girls'
birds' men's flower's
cats' artist's artists'

Page 238
A. (bat's) (teacher's) (sister's)
(store's) (twin's)
bats' teachers' sisters'
stores' twins'

B. 1. teacher's, 2. teachers',
3. bats', 4. bat's, 5. sisters',
6. sister's, 7. stores', 8. store's,
9. twin's, 10. twins'

Page 239
1. b 2. a 3. b 4. c
5. b 6. c 7. a 8. b

Page 240
A. 1. they will 6. you would; you had
2. we are 7. do not
3. it is 8. Manny will
4. have not 9. is not
5. I have 10. who is

B. 1. I'm 5. she's
2. they're 6. he's
3. you've 7. they'll
4. shouldn't 8. aren't

Page 241
A. 1. c 2. g 3. f 4. a
5. h 6. d 7. b 8. e
B. It's, There's, that's, I've, She's, hasn't, you'll, I've, I'll

Page 242
1. b 2. a 3. b 4. b
5. a 6. c 7. b 8. c

Page 244
1. Answers will vary.
2. Answers will vary.
3. Answers will vary.
4. Answers will vary.

Page 246
1. (re)apply, c 6. (in)correct, b
2. (pre)plan, a 7. (dis)obey, c
3. (un)safe, c 8. (im)perfect, b
4. (mis)read, a 9. (over)pay, a
5. (non)stop, a 10. (un)glued, c

Page 247
A. (re)apply (in)direct (re)set
(un)aware (un)known (pre)cut
(in)correct (re)read (pre)plan
(un)happy (pre)pay
(im)proper

B.
pre–	re–	im- or in–	un–
precut	reapply	improper	unaware
prepay	reread	incorrect	unhappy
preplan	reset	indirect	unknown
Answers will vary in last row.			

Page 248
A. (in)complete (pre)pay (pre)views
(im)polite (re)fill (im)perfect
(in)active (un)able

B. 1. impolite, 2. refill, 3. inactive,
4. previews, 5. unable,
6. incomplete, 7. prepay,
8. incorrect

C. unfasten

Page 249
1. c 2. b 3. a 4. c
5. a 6. b 7. b 8. c

Page 250
A. (non)smoking (dis)connect (non)stop
(over)do (over)hear (dis)like
(mis)guide (non)drip (mis)type
(over)throw (mis)name (dis)appear

B.
dis-	mis-	non-	over-
disappear	misguide	nondrip	overdo
disconnect	misname	nonsmoking	overhear
dislike	mistype	nonstop	overthrow
Answers will vary in last row.			

Page 251

A. (circled) disappear, misread, nonsticky, overcharge, disobey, overdue, nonliving, misplace, dislike, nonstop

B. **Across**
1. nonstop
4. disappear
6. misplace
7. overdue
8. dislike

Down
2. nonliving
3. overcharge
5. misread

Page 252
1. a   2. b   3. c   4. a
5. b   6. a   7. c   8. a

Page 254
1. Answers will vary.
2. Answers will vary, such as: So they would be sure to care for Sweetie every day.
3. Answers will vary, such as: responsible; They work as pet sitters.
4. Answers will vary.

Page 255
1. cold**ly** a
2. jogg**er** b
3. funni**est** c
4. water**less** c
5. fix**able** b
6. weak**ness** a
7. round**er** c
8. act**or** a
9. thick**est** c
10. warm**er** b

Page 256

A. visit**or**, thick**er**, sly**ly**, smart**er**, clear**ly**, strang**est**, happ**ier**, silli**est**, train**er**, senat**or**, sweet**est**, teach**er**

B.
–ly	–or or –er	–er	–est
clearly	senator	happier	silliest
slyly	teacher	smarter	strangest
	trainer	thicker	sweetest
	visitor		

Page 257

A. prett**ier**, saf**er**, dark**er**, luck**iest**, loud**ly**, cold**est**, jogg**er**, quiet**ly**, farm**er**, sail**or**

B.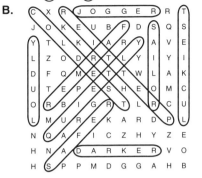

C. Accept any nine words that match the circled words in the puzzle.

Page 258
1. b   2. b   3. a   4. c
5. b   6. c   7. a   8. c

Page 259

A. close**ness**, climb**able**, pain**less**, fair**ness**, bend**able**, point**less**, shy**ness**, enjoy**able**, color**less**, sweet**ness**, drink**able**, blame**less**

B.
–able	–less	–ness
bendable	blameless	closeness
climbable	colorless	fairness
drinkable	painless	shyness
enjoyable	pointless	sweetness
Answers will vary in last row.		

Page 260

A. gentle**ness**, wash**able**, sleep**less**, happi**ness**, thought**less**, ill**ness**, accept**able**, use**less**

B. 1. happiness, 2. thoughtless,
3. washable, 4. illness,
5. useless, 6. gentleness,
7. sleepless, 8. acceptable

C. Answers will vary.

Page 261
1. a   2. b   3. c   4. c
5. a   6. b   7. a   8. b

Page 262

A. back|ground, him|self, out|field, out|doors, rattle|snake, mail|box, day|break, fire|fighter, bed|room, corn|meal, note|book, car|pool

B. 1. f   2. d   3. g   4. a
5. b   6. h   7. e   8. c

Page 263

A. pop|corn, bull|dog, night|time, card|board, fire|fly, hair|cut, oat|meal, birth|day, up|stairs, home|town

B. **Down**
1. nighttime
4. upstairs
5. bulldog
6. popcorn

Across
2. firefly
3. haircut
7. oatmeal
8. cardboard

Page 264
1. c   2. a   3. b   4. c
5. b   6. a   7. c   8. c

Page 266
1. Answers will vary.
2. Answers will vary.
3. The roadrunner would rather walk or run than fly.
4. Answers will vary.
5. No. If a sidewinder had bright-colored skin, Amy and Rick would have seen it in the sand.

Language Fundamentals

Your comprehensive resource for reproducible grade-level grammar, mechanics, and usage practice

The broad scope of language skills and the range of difficulty of the activity pages enable you to precisely target those skills that each student needs to practice. *Language Fundamentals* contains a variety of practice formats. **Correlated to state standards.**

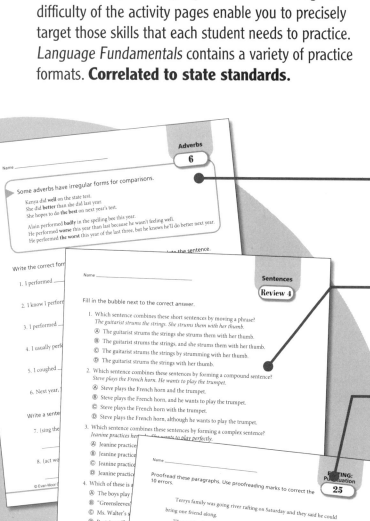

Targeted Skills Practice

The core of *Language Fundamentals* is the 160-plus pages of student-friendly skill activities.

Review Pages

Provides test-prep practice with the multiple-choice format. Reviews follow each small subset of skills.

Sentence or Paragraph Editing

Each page is tied to specific skills addressed in the Targeted Skills Practice pages.

Sentence editing is provided in Grades 1, 2, and 3. Paragraph editing is provided in Grades 4, 5, and 6+.

Language Fundamentals

240 reproducible pages.

Grade 1	EMC 2751	Grade 4	EMC 2754
Grade 2	EMC 2752	Grade 5	EMC 2755
Grade 3	EMC 2753	Grade 6+	EMC 2756

Language Fundamentals
Grade 5 • EMC 2755